THE ULTIMATE
DINOSAUR
ENCYCLOPEDIA

CHRIS BARKER

WELBECK

THIS IS A WELBECK CHILDREN'S BOOK

Text, design and illustration © Welbeck Children's Limited 2020

Published in 2022 by Welbeck Children's Books Limited
An imprint of the Welbeck Publishing Group
Based in London and Sydney.
www.welbeckpublishing.com

A catalogue record for this book is available from the British Library.

ISBN: 978 1 78312 785 6

Printed in Dongguan, China
3 5 7 9 10 8 6 4 2

Author: Chris Barker
Design: Rockjaw Creative
CG Models: Jiří Adamec
Digital Producer: Will Jones
Design Manager: Matt Drew
Editorial Manager: Joff Brown
Production: Nicola Davey

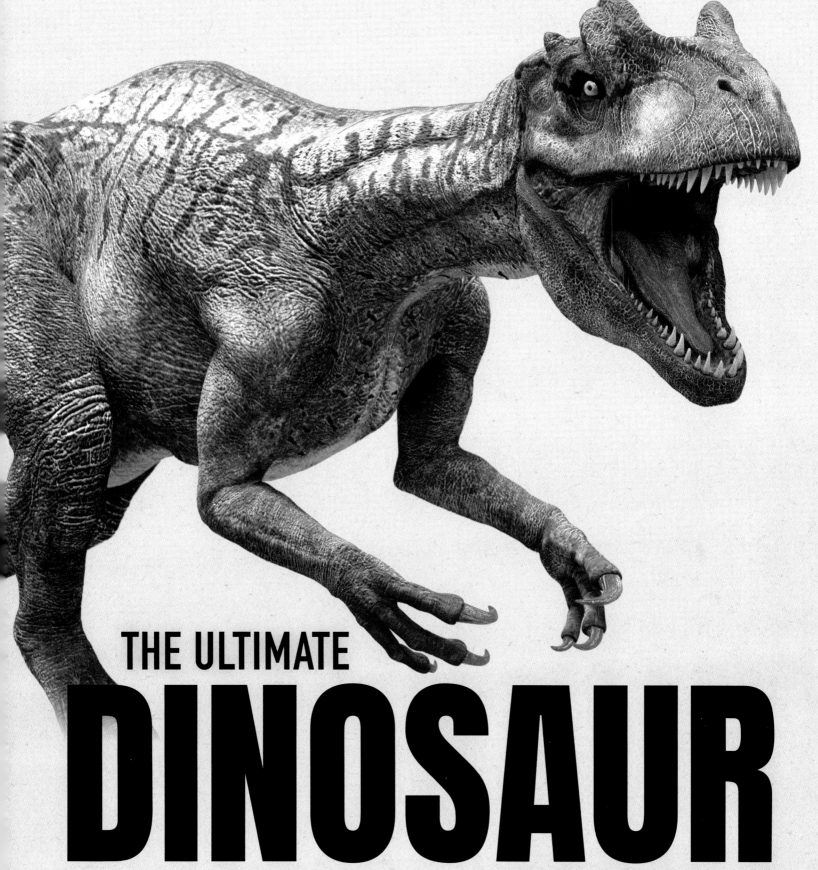

THE ULTIMATE
DINOSAUR
ENCYCLOPEDIA

CHRIS BARKER

CONTENTS

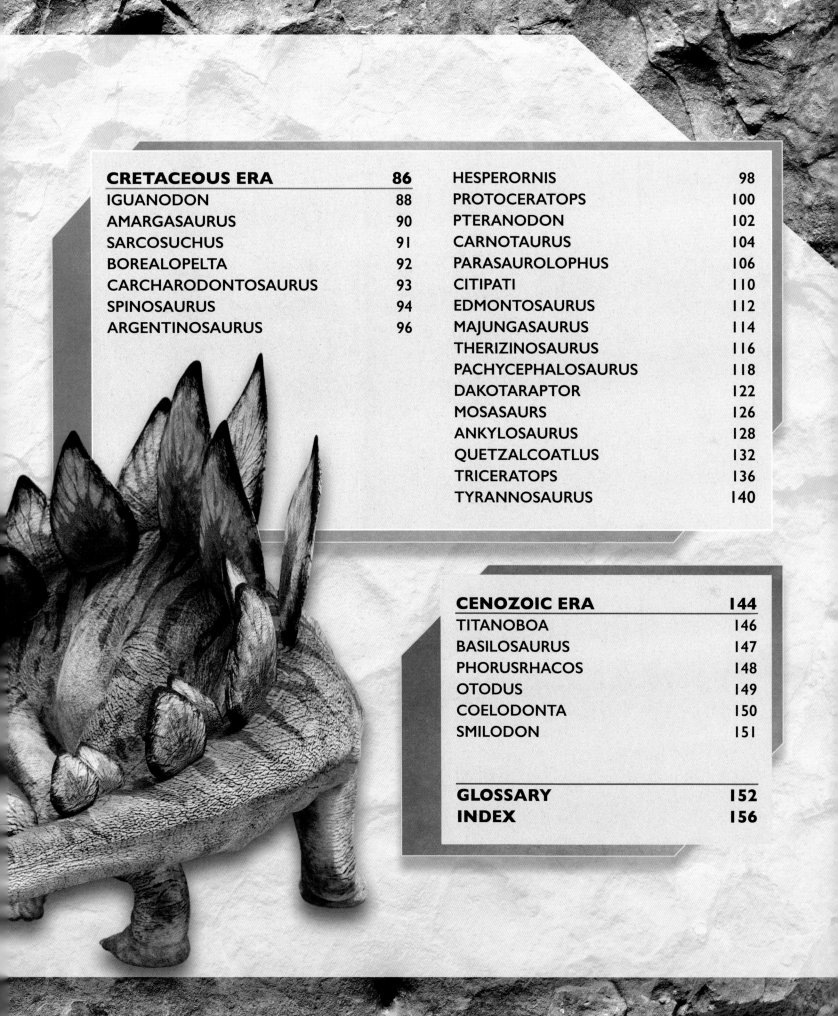

Foreword

Over recent years, our knowledge of prehistoric life has increased by a vast amount. Scientists have discovered hundreds of previously unknown species, have learned a lot about the behavior and biology of extinct animals, and have gained major insight into key evolutionary events. These include the invasion of the land by backboned animals, the rise of dinosaurs, the early history of mammals, and the development and spread of humans and their close hominid relatives.

In this new, lavishly illustrated encyclopedia, you'll learn about gigantic, long-snouted, ancient amphibians, saber-toothed relatives of mammals that ruled the land long before dinosaurs existed, spectacular giant dinosaurs, and the snakes, sharks, birds, and mammals that ruled the world after dinosaurs (excepting birds!) died out.

New, carefully researched illustrations appear throughout this book, and make the images among the most up-to-date and accurate produced so far. We hope you enjoy the ride!

Dr Darren Naish
Zoologist, author, consultant

HOW TO USE THE APP

ACCESSING YOUR BOOK'S ENHANCED DIGITAL FEATURES

1 Download the *Ultimate Dinosaur Encyclopedia* app from the Apple App Store or Google Play, and open it on your smart device.

2 Open the app, then look for the 'SCAN THIS PAGE' icon on the page.

3 View the page through the app, making sure you can see the whole page through the device's screen. You'll see a 3D model of the dinosaur, or an amazing video that plays on the page.

SCAN THIS PAGE TO GET STARTED!

WATCH IT NOW
View this page with in the free app to trigger a video that plays right on the page.

PALEOZOIC ERA

541–252 million years ago

At the beginning of the Paleozoic Era, an amazing event called the Cambrian Explosion sped up the evolution of life on Earth. In the Cambrian Period, many kinds of new creatures developed in the sea, with new abilities like swimming and new body parts like complex eyes.

By the Silurian Period, early plants began their colonisation of land. They provided food for the animals, including insects and primitive vertebrates, that first began to appear in the Devonian Period.

By the Carboniferous Period, the continents of the Earth had merged to form the supercontinent Pangaea. Huge Carboniferous forests were home to diverse forms of terrestrial (land-based) life, including some of the first reptiles. But these rainforest ecosystems collapsed during the Permian Period, the last part of the Paleozoic. Without them, conditions were drier, so some amphibians died out. Reptiles were better adapted to these conditions, and evolved into large herbivores and top carnivores.

There were several mass extinctions in the Paleozoic Era, when thousands of species died out, making way for others who were better adapted to the conditions. The biggest extinction came at the end of the Permian Period, when life on Earth almost became extinct. But a few hardy groups managed to survive into the Mesozoic Era—and one of them would eventually evolve into the mighty dinosaurs.

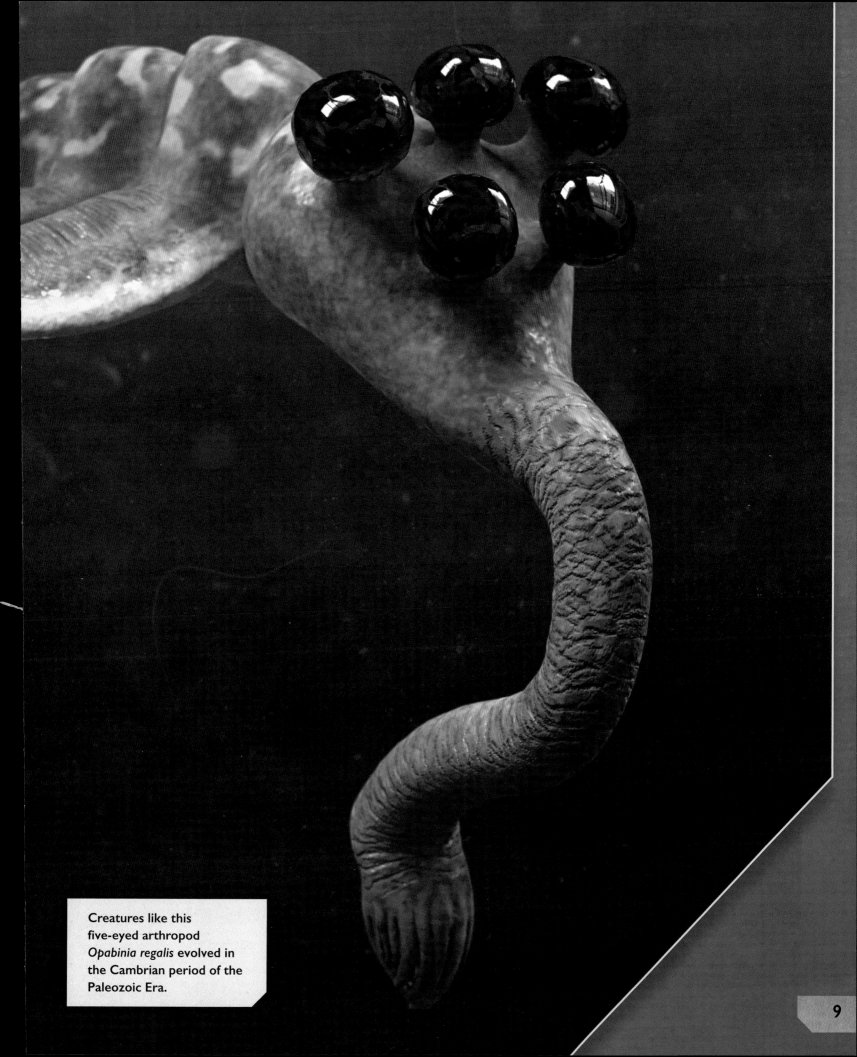

Creatures like this
five-eyed arthropod
Opabinia regalis evolved in
the Cambrian period of the
Paleozoic Era.

EARLY LIFE

The Earth is 4.6 billion years old, and life has probably existed on it for 4 billion years. At the beginning, our planet was a hostile place. Rocks and metals clumped together, forming a dense core and rocky crust, and meteorites bombarded the surface. Yet, as Earth cooled, water began collecting into seas, creating the first habitat for the earliest life.

BILLIONS OF SPECIES

Some scientists estimate that as many as 5 billion species have lived on the Earth since life began. But over 99 percent of them are now extinct.

EARLIEST LIFE

The oceans first formed around 4.41 billion years ago, and some scientists believe that life evolved not long after that. The first organisms would have been single-celled. They may have lived around the super-hot, chemical-rich hydrothermal vents at the bottom of the oceans.

ENERGY FROM THE SUN

Oxygen is a key ingredient for many forms of life. Although 21 percent of our atmosphere is oxygen now, there was none in the air when life began. However, 3.6 billion years ago, a group of simple organisms called **prokaryotes** began harnessing the Sun's light to create energy in a process called **photosynthesis**. Photosynthesis produces oxygen as a waste product, so over hundreds of millions of years, the oxygen levels in the atmosphere increased.

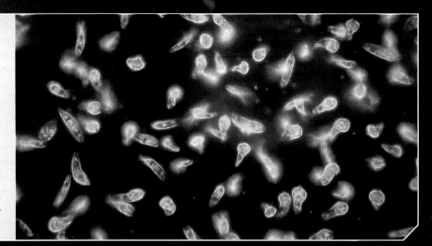

COMPLEX LIFE APPEARS

Over 2 billion years ago, complex single-celled organisms called **eukaryotes** evolved. 300 million years later, these eukaryotes began to group together, forming the first **multicellular organisms**. These complex, multicellular life-forms would eventually evolve and diversify into the animals, plants and fungi that we see today.

THE FIRST ANIMALS

Although life first appeared 4 billion years ago, it wasn't until the Precambrian Era ended, around 600 million years ago, that the first animals evolved. They were possibly just simple, sponge-like creatures. However, during the Cambrian Explosion 50 million years later, complex life diversified into an amazing variety of forms, including most animal groups seen today.

EURYPTERIDS

YOO-rip-TER-rids

Eurypterids are known as "sea scorpions," but they weren't actually scorpions at all. In fact they were aquatic arthropods, who lived in our seas from 460 to 250 million years ago. Some of them grew over 8 ft in length—as long as a polar bear! However, just before the Triassic Period (and the age of the dinosaurs), the eurypterids all died out.

PRIMEVAL PREDATORS

Like many modern arthropods, eurypterids had both complex **compound eyes** to detect movement over a large area, and simpler **ocelli** used to differentiate between light and dark. They could also judge depth, which is important for working out distances when hunting prey. One group, the Pterygotidae, evolved large pincers complete with pointed "teeth" to help grasp prey and move them to the creature's mouth. These animals probably fed on trilobites, jawless fish, and even each other.

One species group, *Eurypterus*, accounts for over 95 percent of all eurypterid specimens known.

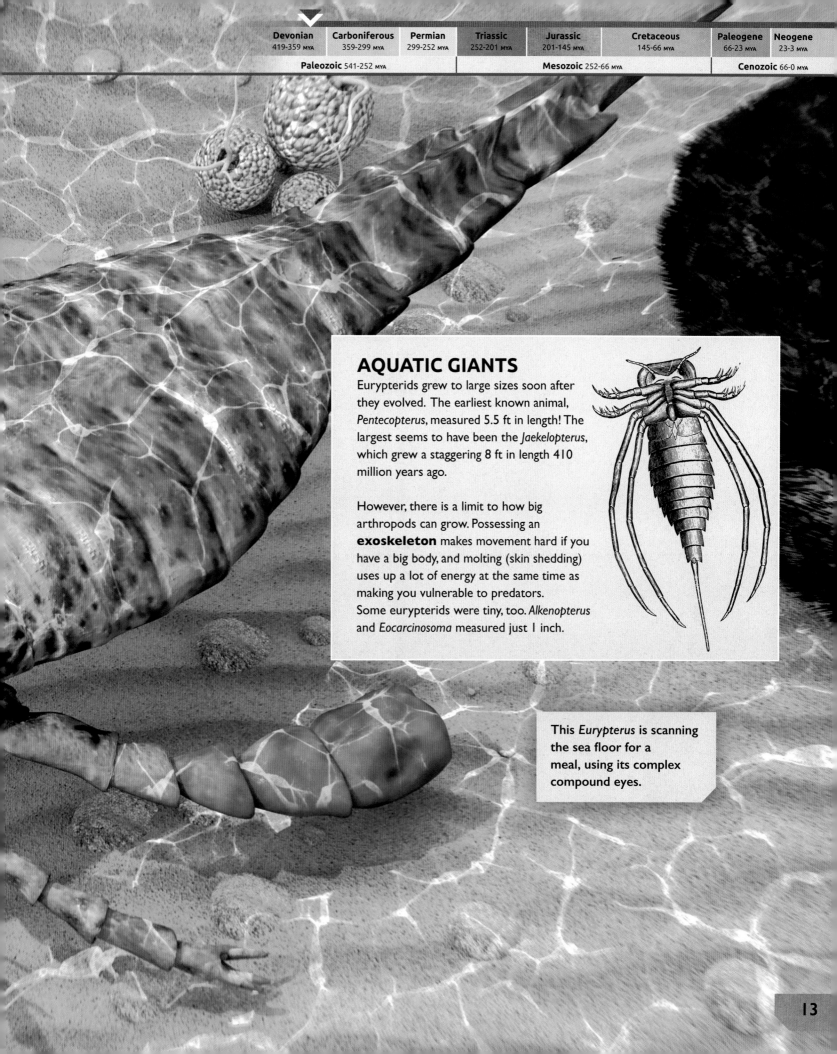

| Devonian 419-359 MYA | Carboniferous 359-299 MYA | Permian 299-252 MYA | Triassic 252-201 MYA | Jurassic 201-145 MYA | Cretaceous 145-66 MYA | Paleogene 66-23 MYA | Neogene 23-3 MYA |

| Paleozoic 541-252 MYA | | | Mesozoic 252-66 MYA | | | Cenozoic 66-0 MYA | |

AQUATIC GIANTS

Eurypterids grew to large sizes soon after they evolved. The earliest known animal, *Pentecopterus*, measured 5.5 ft in length! The largest seems to have been the *Jaekelopterus*, which grew a staggering 8 ft in length 410 million years ago.

However, there is a limit to how big arthropods can grow. Possessing an **exoskeleton** makes movement hard if you have a big body, and molting (skin shedding) uses up a lot of energy at the same time as making you vulnerable to predators. Some eurypterids were tiny, too. *Alkenopterus* and *Eocarcinosoma* measured just 1 inch.

This *Eurypterus* is scanning the sea floor for a meal, using its complex compound eyes.

EARLY VERTEBRATES

Scientists have traced the origins of vertebrates—all animals with backbones—to the Cambrian Explosion, 541 million years ago. However, the exact nature of these origins remains shrouded in mystery, as the closest relatives of vertebrates were soft-bodied organisms whose remains do not fossilise well and are lost to time. As a result, scientists are still debating how the first backboned animals came to be.

VERTEBRATE FEATURES

Vertebrates are often thought of as having a spinal column made of a series of bones, called vertebrae. However, in the first vertebrates, these were basic, and their spinal column was still mostly made of cartilage. The first vertebrates possessed other primitive features like a throat with gill slits, but they also had special features that differentiate them from their later cousins. Recognizable sensory organs, including eyes and ears, all linked to an organized brain, helped form a well-defined head. This head was inherited, and modified, by later vertebrates.

JAWLESS FISH

The most primitive vertebrates are a group of jawless fish known as agnathans ("no jaws"). During the Devonian they were a diverse and numerous group. Some, like the so-called ostracoderms, evolved bony head shields. These shields were made out of many small projections composed of the same materials as teeth. They were attached to an underlying bony plate, and may have had a role in defense. Agnathans probably sucked up food using their throat muscles. By the end of the Devonian, almost all agnathans had become extinct. Hagfish and lampreys are the only ones that survive to this day.

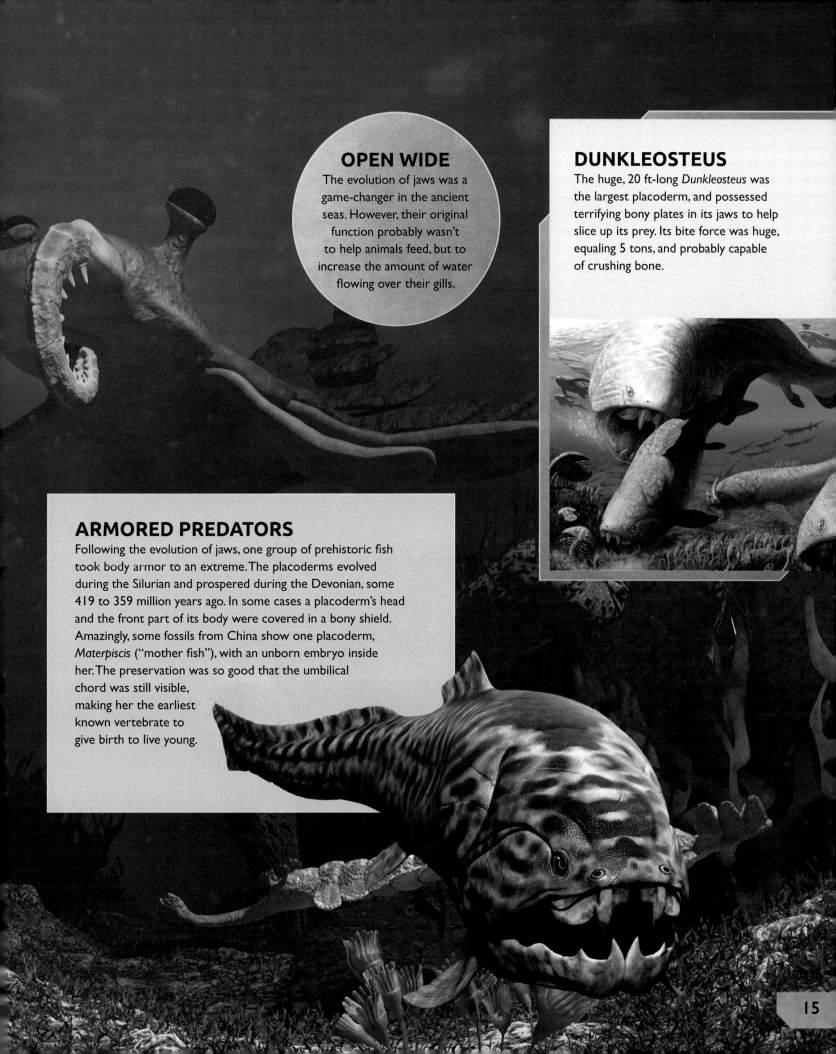

OPEN WIDE
The evolution of jaws was a game-changer in the ancient seas. However, their original function probably wasn't to help animals feed, but to increase the amount of water flowing over their gills.

DUNKLEOSTEUS
The huge, 20 ft-long *Dunkleosteus* was the largest placoderm, and possessed terrifying bony plates in its jaws to help slice up its prey. Its bite force was huge, equaling 5 tons, and probably capable of crushing bone.

ARMORED PREDATORS
Following the evolution of jaws, one group of prehistoric fish took body armor to an extreme. The placoderms evolved during the Silurian and prospered during the Devonian, some 419 to 359 million years ago. In some cases a placoderm's head and the front part of its body were covered in a bony shield. Amazingly, some fossils from China show one placoderm, *Materpiscis* ("mother fish"), with an unborn embryo inside her. The preservation was so good that the umbilical chord was still visible, making her the earliest known vertebrate to give birth to live young.

STETHACANTHUS
Ste-tha-CAN-thus

MEANING: "Chest spine"
PERIOD: Late Devonian to Carboniferous
LOCALITY: Canada
LENGTH: 2.2 ft
WEIGHT: 4.4 lbs
DIET: Fish, crinoids, brachiopods

A mass extinction at the end of the Devonian wiped out entire groups of aquatic organisms. This gave the survivors room to expand. One such group, the stethacanthids, diversified during the Carboniferous. They evolved into bizarre forms like the *Stethacanthus*, a small shark-like marine predator most famous for the bizarre shape on its back, which is known as a spine-brush complex.

FAMILY HISTORY

Despite looking like a small shark, *Stethacanthus* was in fact more closely related to another type of cartilaginous fish: the so-called chimeras. Although just a handful of species of these deep-sea fishes survive today, the group was much more diverse during the Paleozoic.

This shoal of *Stethacanthus* is on the lookout for small fish.

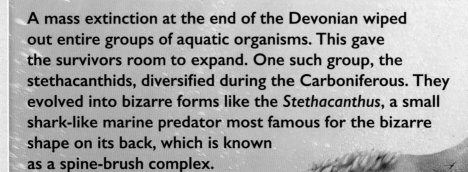

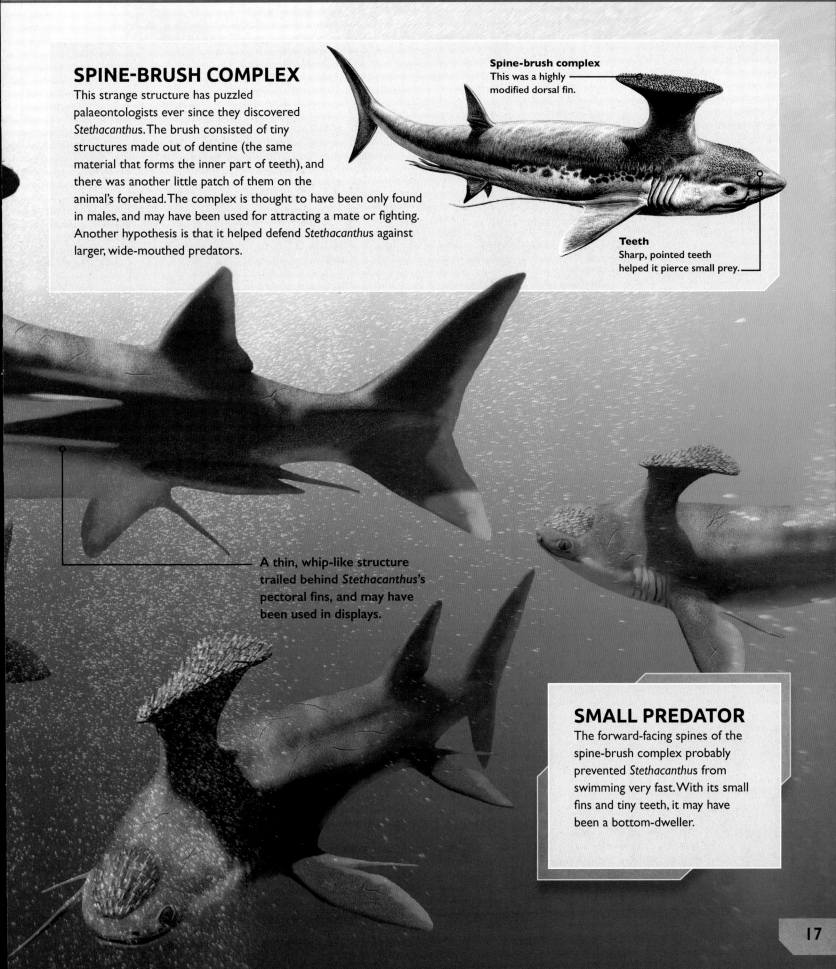

Devonian 419-359 MYA	Carboniferous 359-299 MYA	Permian 299-252 MYA	Triassic 252-201 MYA	Jurassic 201-145 MYA	Cretaceous 145-66 MYA	Paleogene 66-23 MYA	Neogene 23-3 MYA

| Paleozoic 541-252 MYA | | | Mesozoic 252-66 MYA | | | Cenozoic 66-0 MYA | |

SPINE-BRUSH COMPLEX

This strange structure has puzzled palaeontologists ever since they discovered *Stethacanthus*. The brush consisted of tiny structures made out of dentine (the same material that forms the inner part of teeth), and there was another little patch of them on the animal's forehead. The complex is thought to have been only found in males, and may have been used for attracting a mate or fighting. Another hypothesis is that it helped defend *Stethacanthus* against larger, wide-mouthed predators.

Spine-brush complex
This was a highly modified dorsal fin.

Teeth
Sharp, pointed teeth helped it pierce small prey.

A thin, whip-like structure trailed behind *Stethacanthus*'s pectoral fins, and may have been used in displays.

SMALL PREDATOR

The forward-facing spines of the spine-brush complex probably prevented *Stethacanthus* from swimming very fast. With its small fins and tiny teeth, it may have been a bottom-dweller.

17

FIRST TETRAPODS
TET-ra-pods

Tetrapods are four-limbed animals that evolved from a special group of fish known as the "lobe-finned fishes" and appeared as long ago as the Devonian Period. These first tetrapods developed a range of adaptations that helped differentiate them from their aquatic ancestors and allowed their descendants to eventually crawl out of the water and invade terrestrial habitats. Nobody is certain why they made the move, but in their new environment, tetrapods diversified into a huge range of new forms.

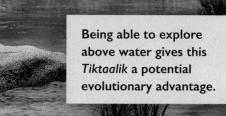

Being able to explore above water gives this *Tiktaalik* a potential evolutionary advantage.

COLONISING LAND
Before true tetrapods dominated terrestrial environments, their close cousins known as tetrapodomorphs evolved important features that they would pass on to the ancestors of modern day amphibians, reptiles, and mammals.

PHASE 1: COMPLETELY AQUATIC
Eusthenopteron (385MYA): This large, fully aquatic lobe-finned fish possessed the same pattern of bones as a tetrapod. Its skeleton featured basic shoulders and a hip girdle as well as primitive arm and leg bones.

PHASE 2: LARGELY AQUATIC

Tiktaalik (375MYA): This animal was still technically a fish, with gills, scales, and fins. However, it evolved a wrist joint and limb bones that allowed it to spend a little time near land. It may have had primitive lungs as well.

WHY DID TETRAPODOMORPHS LEAVE THE WATER?

Scientists are still unsure why tetrapods and their close cousins began moving on to land. Some suggest that their aquatic habitats became unfavorable, forcing them to explore new land-based ecologies that had fewer predators and lots of food.

PHASE 3: SOME TIME ON LAND

Ichthyostega (365MYA): This animal had stronger hips, improving its ability to move on land. Its modified ribs and backbone and its flexible elbow offered extra support too. Nevertheless, *Ichthyostega* still had gills and probably spent most of its time submerged in water, with its eyes and nostrils above the surface.

PHASE 4: A REAL LAND ANIMAL

Ossinodus (333MYA): One of the first true tetrapods and possibly the first truly terrestrial vertebrate, it had strong bones that could bear its weight outside of water. One fossil *Ossinodus* was found to have a half-healed bone fracture that was probably the result of falling from a high place, suggesting it spent a lot of time on land.

HYLONOMUS

High-LON-oh-mus

MEANING: "Forest dweller"
PERIOD: Carboniferous
LOCALITY: Canada
LENGTH: 7.8-9.8 in
WEIGHT: 1.1 lbs
DIET: Insectivore

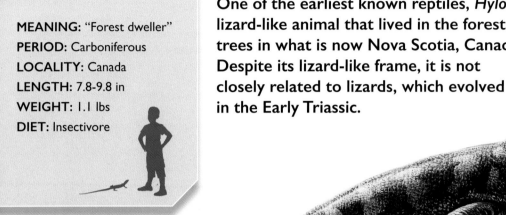

One of the earliest known reptiles, *Hylonomus* was a small, lizard-like animal that lived in the forests of primitive trees in what is now Nova Scotia, Canada. Despite its lizard-like frame, it is not closely related to lizards, which evolved in the Early Triassic.

Like other reptiles, *Hylonomus* had dry, scaly skin.

Hylonomus fossils have sometimes been found in fossil tree stumps.

GIANT ARTHROPODS

Not all arthropods were on *Hylonomus'* menu. Because of the high oxygen levels during the Carboniferous, some arthropods grew to very large sizes. Twenty-inch-wide tracks made by the giant millipede *Arthropleura* have been discovered near where *Hylonomus* lived. Luckily for the little reptile, these huge arthropods were herbivorous.

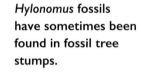

INSECT-EATER

Hylonomus' lightly built skull and small, sharp teeth were perfect for capturing insects and other arthropods, while its lizard-like body helped it scamper around its forest habitat.

Devonian 419-359 MYA	Carboniferous 359-299 MYA	Permian 299-252 MYA	Triassic 252-201 MYA	Jurassic 201-145 MYA	Cretaceous 145-66 MYA	Paleogene 66-23 MYA	Neogene 23-3 MYA
Paleozoic 541-252 MYA			Mesozoic 252-66 MYA			Cenozoic 66-0 MYA	

PRIONOSUCHUS

Pry-ONO-sook-hus

MEANING: "Prion crocodile"
PERIOD: Early Permian
LOCALITY: Brazil
LENGTH: 9-29 ft
WEIGHT: 2.2 tons
DIET: Fish and amphibians

Despite its looks, the giant *Prionosuchus* was not a crocodile. In fact, it wasn't even a reptile, but part of a group of amphibians called temnospondyls. While most specimens measured around 9 ft in length, fragmentary remains suggest the largest individuals could reach 29 ft, with skulls measuring up to 5 ft long.

CONVERGENT EVOLUTION

Prionosuchus is only a distant relation of modern crocodiles. Their similar looks and features are an example of **convergent evolution**, where two distantly related organisms evolve similar traits to do similar jobs or adapt to similar environments. *Prionosuchus* spent a lot of time in the water and so do crocodiles, so they both independently evolved long snouts and streamlined bodies, which are good for catching fish.

The rocks in which *Prionosuchus* was found show that it lived in fresh water, most probably a system of deep rivers and lakes.

Despite its large skull, *Prionosuchus* had small arms and legs—the thighbone of the largest fossil specimen measures just 5 inches long!

Devonian 419-359 MYA	Carboniferous 359-299 MYA	Permian 299-252 MYA	Triassic 252-201 MYA	Jurassic 201-145 MYA	Cretaceous 145-66 MYA	Paleogene 66-23 MYA	Neogene 23-3 MYA
Paleozoic 541-252 MYA			Mesozoic 252-66 MYA			Cenozoic 66-0 MYA	

DIMETRODON

Dy-MET-ro-don

MEANING: "Two measures
of teeth"
PERIOD: Early Permian
LOCALITY: USA, Germany
LENGTH: 5.6-15 ft
WEIGHT: 61-110 lbs
DIET: Carnivore

The impressive sail-backed *Dimetrodon* was a top
predator in North America and Europe almost 300
million years ago. Despite its dinosaurian appearance,
it belongs to a group of animals called synapsids and
is more closely related to mammals than to dinosaurs
or any living reptile. Scientists are still debating the
exact function of the huge sail along its back.

SAIL-BACKED PREDATOR

The sail was covered by a thin membrane,
although the tips of the spines may have been
exposed. As for its function, scientists used
to think it radiated heat like an elephant's
ear, preventing *Dimetrodon* from overheating.
Some more recent ideas are that it helped the
creature keep its balance when walking, or
helped attract a mate.

UPRIGHT GAIT?

Since its discovery in
the late 19th century,
Dimetrodon has often been
drawn creeping along with
its belly to the ground,
dragging its tail. However,
recent analysis of some
footprints suggests it could
stand much more upright
when it wanted to.

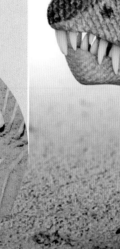

ANCIENT ARMS RACE

Dimetrodon is one of the earliest known terrestrial carnivores with serrated teeth, which helped it slice through flesh. However, the teeth of older species have straight cutting edges, which are much better for dealing with small prey. *Dimetrodon* species may have gradually evolved to tackle larger and larger prey.

Dimetrodon's legs were probably strong enough to keep its body off the ground.

GORGONOPSIA

GOR-gon-OP-sia

The gorgonopsia were some of the largest predators to prowl the middle to late Permian, 270 to 252 million years ago. These four-legged carnivores weren't dinosaurs, but therapsids, related to mammals. While most gorgonopsians were rather small, with skulls roughly 6 inches long, by the late Permian some had reached bear-sized proportions, allowing them to tackle big prey species.

Scientists are unsure whether gorgonopsia were furry or hairless.

MOVING AROUND

Gorgonopsians had a more upright stance compared to their reptilian ancestors, and they did not move their body from side to side when they walked. This gait allowed them to be more active, improving their speed, and as a result they were probably adept at outrunning slower prey.

A PREDATOR'S BRAIN

Palaeontologists have been able to reconstruct the brains of gorgonopsians. In some species, the area of the brain that helps stabilize the head and eyes when tracking objects is rather large, which might have been useful when hunting prey.

The creature had a small brain, similar to that of its reptilian ancestors.

KILLER JAWS

Gorgonopsians had several different kinds of teeth, like mammals: incisors at the front, huge, saber-tooth canines just behind them, and post-canine teeth at the rear. However, these were continually replaced throughout life, just like reptiles' teeth. They also had several biting styles: they could open their jaws up to 90 degrees, letting their canines sink into prey, or they could slide their incisors past each other for smaller, jagged bites.

LYSTROSAURUS
LIS-tro-SOR-us

This pig-sized herbivore was found all over the globe, and it was a great survivor. At the end of the Permian Period, 252 million years ago, the worst mass extinction in the history of the planet occurred. Around 96 percent of life died out. *Lystrosaurus* was one of the rare creatures that managed to survive into the Triassic.

Lystrosaurus was perhaps a relatively social animal, living in small herds that may have helped protect individuals from predators.

POST-EXTINCTION WORLD

During the Early Triassic, the Earth was recovering from a devastating mass extinction. The disapperance of several major terrestrial species meant that the surviving species of *Lystrosaurus* could occupy the empty niches they left behind. A niche is the role of an organism within an ecosystem. *Lystrosaurus*' numbers exploded, and some palaeontologists have suggested this herbivore made up 95 percent of all terrestrial vertebrates for a short while.

Well-preserved fossils such as this skull are quite common and provide plenty of information about *Lystrosaurus*' anatomy.

KEEN BURROWER

Muscular forelimbs and short, robust tusks helped make *Lystrosaurus* an excellent digger, and it may have lived underground. Some burrows have been found with the animals still in them. However, a few researchers have suggested these dens may have actually belonged to predators, and the *Lystrosaurus* were placed there as a snack for later.

MAMMALIAN COUSIN

Lystrosaurus belongs to the dicynodont therapsids, a group of animals closely related to mammals. But unlike most modern mammals, *Lystrosaurus* moved around with a semi-sprawling gait. Its skeleton was adapted in a number of ways to prevent too much side-to-side movement.

TRIASSIC ERA

252–202 million years ago

In the Triassic Era, the continents were still locked in the giant landmass Pangaea, and the center of the supercontinent received very little rain. The climate was warm throughout the Triassic, and life was still recovering from the devastating extinction that had occurred at the end of the Permian. However, the lack of competitors meant the survivors could move into all sorts of empty niches. Some reptiles returned to the sea, evolving into the dolphin-like ichthyosaurs and long-necked plesiosaurs. In the air, pterosaurs joined the insects and became the first flying vertebrates.

Life on land was marked by the dominance of one group of reptiles: the archosaurs. These "ruling reptiles" were highly successful, and one group in particular—the predatory relatives of modern crocodilians—sat at the top of the food chain. Meanwhile, some relics from the Permian still persisted, like the dicynodonts. These herbivorous relatives of modern mammals were present all over Pangaea, some of them growing to huge sizes.

It wasn't until the Late Triassic that the first dinosaurs appeared, and even then they weren't the dominant archosaur group on land. Luckily for dinosaurs, another mass extinction at the end of the Triassic wiped out their competitors. They were able to diversify and become the dominant land vertebrate for the remainder of the Mesozoic.

RISE OF THE DINOSAURS

The Permian-Triassic Mass Extinction 252 years ago caused the most devastating extinction ever, with a cataclysmic loss of biodiversity. Fortunately, the early Triassic was a time of recovery and experimentation for the survivors. One group of reptiles, the archosaurs, would go on to be extremely successful, evolving into many lineages ... one of which eventually gave rise to the dinosaurs.

RULING REPTILES

The name archosaur means "ruling reptile," and for good reason: this group of reptiles was very successful during the Mesozoic, overtaking the synapsids as the dominant terrestrial vertebrate. Archosaurs can be split into two major lineages: the pseudosuchians, made up of the crocodilians and all their extinct ancestors, and the avemetatarsalians, which included the flying pterosaurs as well as the dinosaurs. Birds, being living dinosaurs, also belong to this second group.

The Permian-Triassic Mass Extinction allowed archosaurs to flourish, eventually leading to the rule of dinosaurs in the Jurassic and Cretaceous.

LUCKY DINOSAURS?

The Triassic is known as the beginning of the dinosaur era. However, dinosaurs only began to evolve late in the period, and for a long time the pseudosuchians were far more abundant and diverse. However, two small extinction events at the end of the Triassic wiped out almost all pseudosuchians, leaving the lucky dinosaur survivors to rapidly evolve and replace them.

Climate change caused by long-term volcanic activity may have caused the Permian-Triassic Mass Extinction event.

RECOVERING EARTH

For a long time, the reasons behind the mass extinction at the end of the Permian were unclear. However, recent research points to climate change caused by long-term volcanic activity, increasing the temperature of air and seas over hundreds of thousands of years, as the major killer. Incredibly, 70 percent of terrestrial species and 95 percent of marine species vanished forever. Humans today are currently increasing global temperatures at similar rates—a major cause for concern.

WHAT IS A DINOSAUR?

Dinosaurs evolved from a group of archosaurs known as dinosauriformes during the Late Triassic, around 240-235 million years ago. The primitive dinosauriformes, such as the silesaurids, were very closely related, but lacked certain characteristics seen in the more advanced "true" dinosaurs, and became extinct by the end of the Triassic. All dinosaurs share a range of anatomical traits that unite them, but the group is split into a several different lineages, and the shape of the dinosaur family tree may change with new discoveries.

TRADTIONAL FAMILY TREE

The standard version of the dinosaur family tree splits them into two groups: the saurischians and the ornithischians. This is based on the shape of their hips, but there are several other traits that help distinguish between the two.

SAURISCHIANS: The "lizard-hipped" dinosaurs have one hipbone facing forward, and another facing backward, similar to reptiles. However, like modern birds, not all of them had this configuration.

ORNITHISCHIANS: The "bird-hipped" dinosaurs were not actually the ancestors of modern birds. However, like birds, they had hipbones that faced backwards. This might have made more space for their guts, to help them digest plant matter. They also had an additional bone at the tip of their lower jaw.

A NEW TREE?

Recently some scientists have suggested that the traditional view of dinosaur evolution is incorrect. By looking closely at the anatomy of dinosaurs at the bottom of the family tree, they discovered that the theropods and ornithischians were closely related, forming a group called Ornithoscelida. They appear to have shared over twenty (sometimes subtle) traits, including similarities in the skull, vertebrae, and shin bones.

Sauropodomorphs: Some of the largest animals to ever walk the Earth, these are recognizable by their long necks and tails. Early sauropodomorphs were bipedal.

Theropods: These were generally bipedal carnivores, although some did evolve to eat plants. The evolution of the theropods would eventually lead to birds.

Birds: All modern birds are descended from theropods.

Marginocephalians: The earliest forms were small bipeds. However, they later became quadrupeds and evolved massive frilled or domed skulls.

Ornithopods: This group includes some crested forms that possessed jaws lined with hundreds of plant-crushing teeth.

CERAPODANS

Stegosaurs: These herbivores possessed massive spikes and plates running down their backs or jutting out of their shoulders.

Ankylosaurs: These tank-like herbivores were well armored and had a range of clubs, spikes, and bony knobs to protect against predators.

THYREOPHORANS

HERRERASAURUS

He-RER-ra-SOR-rus

MEANING: "Herrera's lizard"
PERIOD: Late Triassic
LOCALITY: South America
LENGTH: 9-19 ft
WEIGHT: 771 lbs
DIET: Carnivore

Herrerasaurus was one of the first dinosaurs to evolve, and also one of the largest during the Late Triassic. Although its rectangular skull was primitive compared to those of later dinosaurs, it was an active predator, prowling the ancient forests and floodplains of what is now Argentina.

This reconstruction of *Herrerasaurus* shows how it stood upright on strong legs and balanced itself with its tail.

TRIASSIC SQUABBLES

One *Herrerasaurus* was found with bite marks in its skull that had given it a small infection, but left it alive. A massive crocodilian relative, *Saurosuchus*, was found fossilized in the same formation, but its large and powerful jaws would probably have killed *Herrerasaurus*. Instead, the small injury seems to have been dealt by another of its kind. Perhaps they were fighting over food or territory.

Devonian	Carboniferous	Permian	Triassic	Jurassic	Cretaceous	Paleogene	Neogene
419-359 MYA	359-299 MYA	299-252 MYA	252-201 MYA	201-145 MYA	145-66 MYA	66-23 MYA	23-3 MYA

| Paleozoic 541-252 MYA | | | Mesozoic 252-66 MYA | | | Cenozoic 66-0 MYA | |

UNCERTAIN RELATIONS

Herrerasaurus and its closest relatives are usually considered to be theropods. After all, they shared their basic body plan, curved teeth, and bipedal gait with other theropod dinosaurs. However, recent research suggests they may have been more closely related to sauropods.

The creature's slender, flexible neck allowed it to whip its head around quickly and grab prey.

FLEXIBLE JAW

Herrerasaurus' lower jaw had a joint that allowed extra flexibility within the mandible beyond the usual up and down motion. Some modern lizards have this additional jaw joint, and it may help their front teeth to rotate a little, which could be useful in capturing prey.

35

EORAPTOR

Ey-OH-rap-tor

MEANING: "Dawn thief"
PERIOD: Late Triassic
LOCALITY: South America
LENGTH: 3 ft
WEIGHT: 22 lbs
DIET: Omnivore

One of the most primitive dinosaurs yet discovered, the carnivorous little *Eoraptor* scurried around what is now Argentina in the Late Triassic Period, keeping a watchful eye out for larger predators such as *Saurosuchus* and *Herrerasaurus*.

TAIL
The long tail helped the bipedal *Eoraptor* maintain balance.

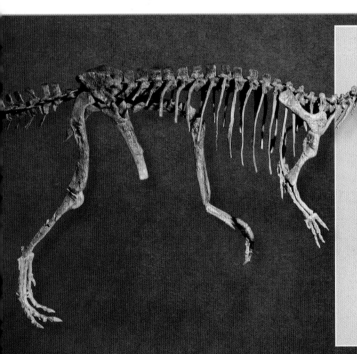

PRIMITIVE DINOSAUR

Eoraptor shares lots of traits in common with both the sauropods and the theropods. Scientists debate whether it is truly a sauropod, a theropod or a primitive saurischian (the larger category that includes both of the previous groups).

Its lightweight body frame made *Eoraptor* a swift sprinter.

TEETH
Eoraptor's teeth were specialized for a wide-ranging diet (see below).

HIND LEGS
Eoraptor ran digitigrade, meaning it balanced on the end of its hindleg digits.

BROAD DIET

Eoraptor's teeth were heterodont, meaning they were different shapes and therefore had different functions. The back half of its upper jaw was full of curved, serrated teeth, like those of carnivorous theropods, while the front half housed leaf-shaped teeth like those of sauropodomorphs. This suggests it was capable of feeding on both plants and prey.

Sharp claws and flexible elbows allowed it to grab and hold prey.

PLATEOSAURUS

PLAT-ee-o-SOR-us

MEANING: "Broad lizard"
PERIOD: Late Triassic
LOCALITY: Europe
LENGTH: 13-32 ft
WEIGHT: 1,388-8,800 lbs
DIET: Herbivore

Many complete skeletons of this European dinosaur have been found, allowing palaeontologists to study and understand the animal's biology in great detail. With its long neck and tail, it was an early sauropodomorph, but unlike its later cousins, it was bipedal. It was a common dinosaur during the Late Triassic period.

A thick, muscular tail helped balance the body as it moved around on its hind limbs.

BIRDLIKE LUNGS

Scientists think *Plateosaurus* had birdlike lungs that supplied its body with plenty of oxygen to fuel its growth and activity, as well as birdlike joints between the ribs and vertebrae. New evidence suggests some of these traits can be traced back to the dinosauriformes, and may have contributed to the diversification of the dinosaurs during the Mesozoic.

While its skull was generally similar in shape to later herbivores like *Stegosaurus*, its bite force was not as high, so it might have preferred to eat softer vegetation.

GROWING UP

When you look at them under a microscope, dinosaur bones often show rings that allow scientists to calculate their age and growth rates, like tree rings. Fossilized *Plateosaurus* bones show the typical fast growth seen in other dinosaurs and mammals, but their size was still very dependent on environmental factors such as the availability of food. Because of this, individuals of similar ages differed in size.

THE GAIT DEBATE

Some palaeontologists used to think that *Plateosaurus* walked on four legs. However, modern techniques using 3D models and computer software have shown that this would be impractical, and the animal probably moved comfortably on two legs. However, its maximum speed never exceeded a fast walk. It may have used its arms to help gather food, or during fights with other *Plateosaurus*.

Footprints of a *Plateosaurus*-like dinosaur support the suggestion that these animals walked on two legs.

PSEUDOSUCHIANS

SOO-doe-SOO-kee-ans

The pseudosuchians were extremely successful during the Triassic—far more so than the dinosaurs—and evolved into a vast array of different forms and lifestyles. Yet, for reasons that are still not entirely clear, few pseudosuchians survived the extinction event at the end of the Triassic era. Those that did eventually evolved into the crocodilians we know today.

PSEUDOSUCHIAN TRAITS

Although they look very much like dinosaurs, one of the major differences between the pseudosuchians and their dinosaur and pterosaur cousins was the anatomy of their ankle joints. Their anklebones were able to rotate relative to one another, meaning that the pseudosuchians could have either a sprawling or a more upright stance. Dinosaurs and pterosaurs had a simple hinge for an ankle, restricting their posture to an upright stance.

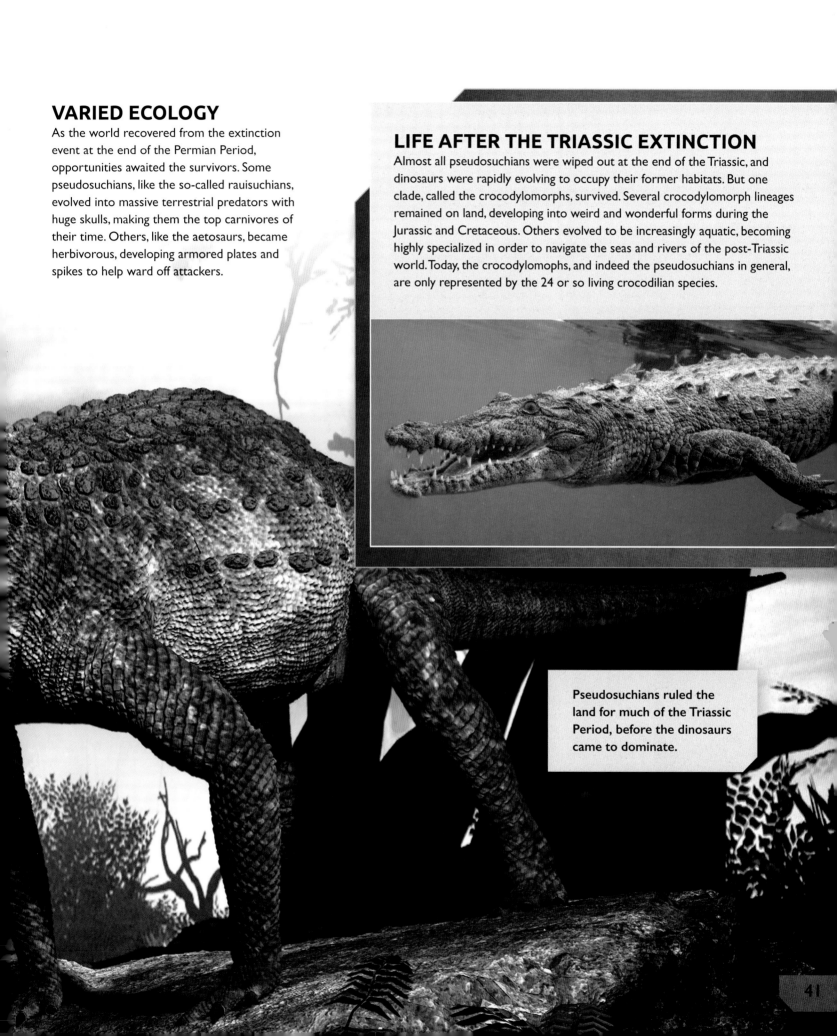

VARIED ECOLOGY

As the world recovered from the extinction event at the end of the Permian Period, opportunities awaited the survivors. Some pseudosuchians, like the so-called rauisuchians, evolved into massive terrestrial predators with huge skulls, making them the top carnivores of their time. Others, like the aetosaurs, became herbivorous, developing armored plates and spikes to help ward off attackers.

LIFE AFTER THE TRIASSIC EXTINCTION

Almost all pseudosuchians were wiped out at the end of the Triassic, and dinosaurs were rapidly evolving to occupy their former habitats. But one clade, called the crocodylomorphs, survived. Several crocodylomorph lineages remained on land, developing into weird and wonderful forms during the Jurassic and Cretaceous. Others evolved to be increasingly aquatic, becoming highly specialized in order to navigate the seas and rivers of the post-Triassic world. Today, the crocodylomophs, and indeed the pseudosuchians in general, are only represented by the 24 or so living crocodilian species.

Pseudosuchians ruled the land for much of the Triassic Period, before the dinosaurs came to dominate.

POSTOSUCHUS

POST-oh-SOO-kus

MEANING: "Crocodile from Post" (a place in Texas, USA)
PERIOD: Late Triassic
LOCALITY: North America
LENGTH: 16-19 ft
WEIGHT: 550-600 lbs
DIET: Carnivore

Although it looked very much like a predatory dinosaur, *Postosuchus* was in fact a large terrestrial pseudosuchian that enjoyed life at the top of the Late Triassic food chain. Solidly built, with a 21-inch-long skull, *Postosuchus* made easy work of the smaller dinosaurs of its time.

A double row of osteoderms—bones embedded in the skin—covered its back and tail and may have protected it from other *Postosuchus*.

GUT CONTENTS

The preserved stomach contents of one *Postosuchus* showed its varied diet. Four different animals were found in its ribcage, including a herbivorous pseudosuchian, two synapsids, and a type of amphibian! What's more, the *Postosuchus* was found on top of a *Dromicosuchus*, a primitive relative of modern-day crocodilians. The *Dromicosuchus* also had bite marks in its skull, suggesting the *Postosuchus* attacked it before both suddenly died, either as result of fighting or some other cause.

UPRIGHT STANCE

Scientists used to believe that *Postosuchus* moved around on all fours. However, better-preserved fossils show that its arms were short and its hands were roughly a third of the size of its feet. This would have made *Postosuchus* stalk around on its hind legs instead.

TOUGH LIFE AT THE TOP

Just because an organism is at the top of the food chain doesn't mean it's safe from danger. Two huge thighbones, possibly belonging to *Postosuchus*, were found showing evidence of severe injury. One had a tooth embedded in it, though the victim had survived the attack. The other showed unhealed bite marks, suggesting the victim either died soon after being bitten, or was scavenged. Analysis of the teeth and bite pattern suggest that the attacker was a phytosaur, a type of semi-aquatic archosaur.

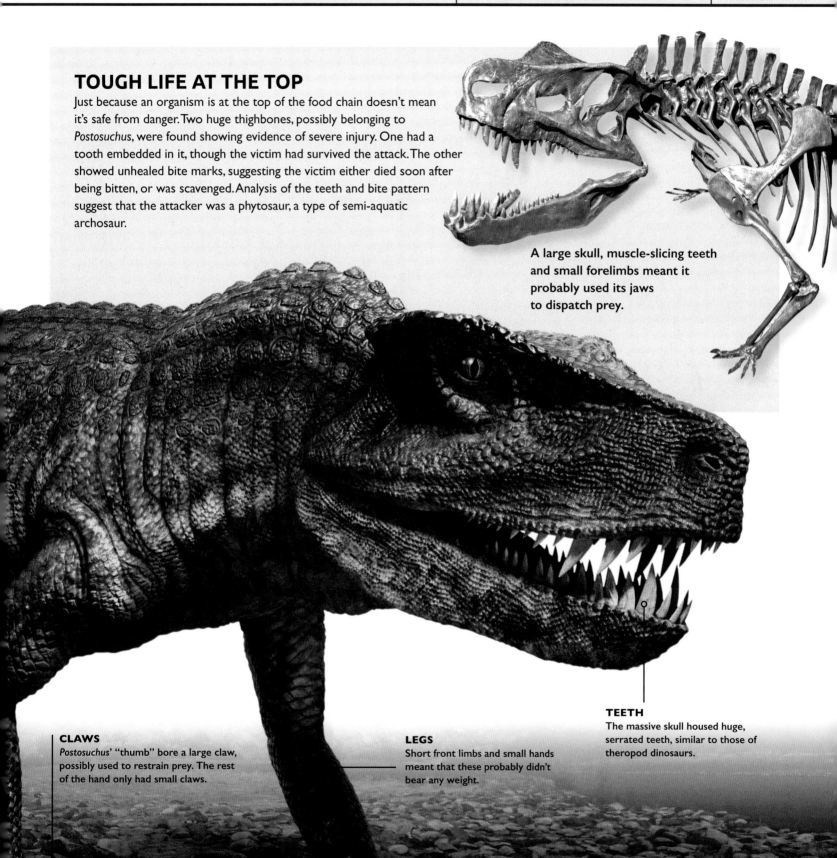

A large skull, muscle-slicing teeth and small forelimbs meant it probably used its jaws to dispatch prey.

CLAWS
Postosuchus' "thumb" bore a large claw, possibly used to restrain prey. The rest of the hand only had small claws.

LEGS
Short front limbs and small hands meant that these probably didn't bear any weight.

TEETH
The massive skull housed huge, serrated teeth, similar to those of theropod dinosaurs.

43

DESMATOSUCHUS

DES-mat-oh-SOO-kus

MEANING: "Link crocodile"
PERIOD: Late Triassic
LOCALITY: North America
LENGTH: 13-19 ft
WEIGHT: 617-837 lbs
DIET: Herbivore

These bulky herbivores belonged to a group of pseudosuchians known as the aetosaurs. *Desmatosuchus* in particular is famous for its heavily armored, spiny skin. A double row of osteoderms lined its back, with their spiked ends facing outward protecting the neck and body. Most impressive were its huge, curved "shoulder" spikes, which had evolved for good reason: *Desmatosuchus* shared an environment with the equally huge *Postosuchus*.

Bulldozing its way through the dry undergrowth, this *Desmatosuchus* has spent most of the day foraging in order to fuel its bulk.

SOCIAL REPTILE?

The discovery of several *Desmatosuchus* fossilized remains close to one another led some scientists to argue that these herbivores lived in groups. However, these boneyards also contained a range of other vertebrates, so it's possible that all the bodies just washed into the same place after death. The only fossilized *Desmatosuchus* tracks yet found show the animals moving alone.

Devonian	Carboniferous	Permian	Triassic	Jurassic	Cretaceous	Paleogene	Neogene
419-359 MYA	359-299 MYA	299-252 MYA	252-201 MYA	201-145 MYA	145-66 MYA	66-23 MYA	23-3 MYA

Paleozoic 541-252 MYA	Mesozoic 252-66 MYA	Cenozoic 66-0 MYA

FOOD FOR THOUGHT

What exactly did *Desmatosuchus* (as well as other aetosaurs) eat? Some scientists think it was an insectivore, due to some similarities with modern day armadillos: the tip of its jaw was toothless, and its upturned snout might have been good for digging. However, it had fewer teeth than its ancestors, which is usually a feature of animals evolving toward a plant-based diet, and the position of its jaw joint is similar to that of known herbivores. *Desmatosuchus* was also capable of slow, high-force bites, perhaps to crush tough plant matter.

While the shoulder spikes might have been useful for warning predators, they might have also been used to attract mates.

OTHER TRIASSIC LIFE

With so many habitats and niches left open following the Permian extinction, the Triassic was a time of experimentation and diversification. Some creatures would go on to thrive during the Mesozoic, but for others, the Triassic mass extinction was the end of the line.

TERRESTRIAL

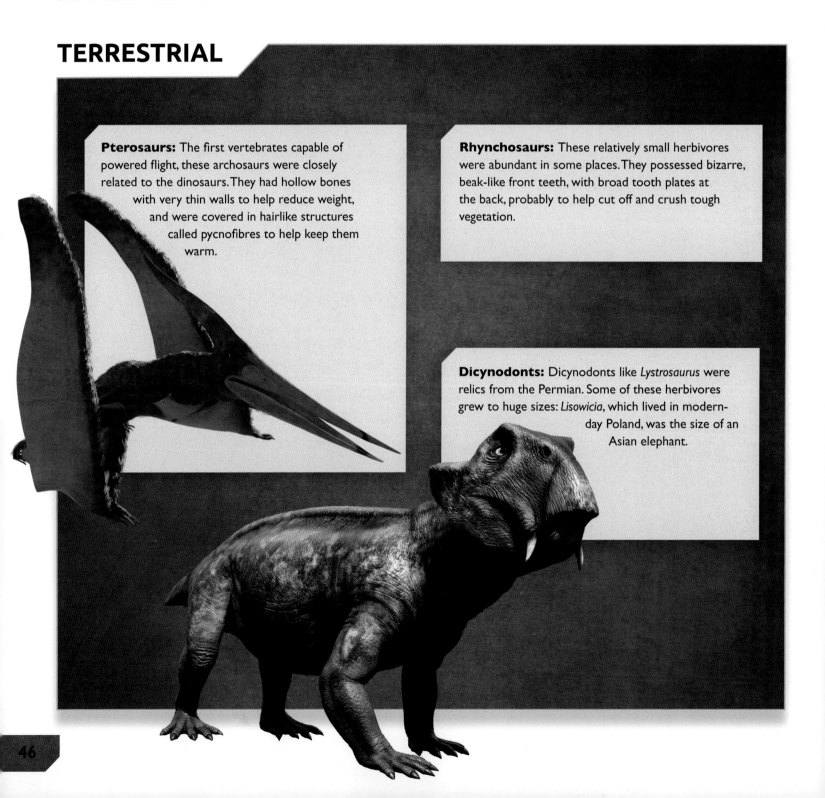

Pterosaurs: The first vertebrates capable of powered flight, these archosaurs were closely related to the dinosaurs. They had hollow bones with very thin walls to help reduce weight, and were covered in hairlike structures called pycnofibres to help keep them warm.

Rhynchosaurs: These relatively small herbivores were abundant in some places. They possessed bizarre, beak-like front teeth, with broad tooth plates at the back, probably to help cut off and crush tough vegetation.

Dicynodonts: Dicynodonts like *Lystrosaurus* were relics from the Permian. Some of these herbivores grew to huge sizes: *Lisowicia*, which lived in modern-day Poland, was the size of an Asian elephant.

AQUATIC

Ichthyosaurs: The ichthyosaurs evolved from semi-aquatic ancestors and thrived in the Triassic seas. Some grew huge, such as *Shastasaurus*, which reached 68 ft long. Their bodies were very streamlined to help them swim after prey and away from predators.

Nothosaurs: These reptiles had jaws full of sharp, outwardly pointing teeth. Their flexible necks and flipper-like hands helped them chase after small fish and squid. They were related to the plesiosaurs, which eventually replaced them at the end of the Triassic.

Placodonts: The large, flat teeth of most placodonts meant they were well equipped for dealing with hard, shelled prey. *Henodus* evolved fine denticles in its jaws to help filter out tiny invertebrates from the water. Placodonts probably lived in shallow, coastal seas.

SEMI-AQUATIC

Phytosaurs: These lived in watery habitats and resembled modern-day crocodiles, but they are only distantly related. Phytosaurs had serrated teeth, suggesting they did not engage in a "death-roll" when feeding, as modern crocodiles do to bite off chunks of flesh.

TANYSTROPHEUS

TAN-ee-STRO-fee-us

MEANING: "Long-hinged"
PERIOD: Middle Triassic
LOCALITY: Europe, Israel, China
LENGTH: 11-19 ft
WEIGHT: 66-220 lbs
DIET: Carnivore

The mysterious *Tanystropheus* was closely related to the archosaurs, possessing a very long neck and small front limbs. It was originally described as a type of pterosaur, and many details of its anatomy and lifestyle continue to puzzle scientists today.

Tanystropheus has been mainly found in two types of deposits: shallow marine environments, and coastal rivers, lakes, and lagoons.

EXTREME NECK

Tanystropheus' small head was perched on a slender neck made up of about a dozen elongated vertebrae. It may have been useful for sneaking up on aquatic prey without them noticing *Tanystropheus'* body. Some previous reconstructions suggested the neck was too heavy and awkward to be used on land, but as there was little muscle surrounding the vertebrae, the neck might have been light enough to have supported the head on land.

WAS IT A GOOD SWIMMER?

Its tail was short and not well adapted to propel the animal through water, while its hands and feet were not flipper-shaped. In addition, its limb bones were hollow, which would have made it hard for the creature to dive. Instead, it appears that this predator may have used its long neck as a crane, possibly to catch small prey both in water and on land.

	Devonian 419-359 MYA	Carboniferous 359-299 MYA	Permian 299-252 MYA	Triassic 252-201 MYA	Jurassic 201-145 MYA	Cretaceous 145-66 MYA	Paleogene 66-23 MYA	Neogene 23-3 MYA
	Paleozoic 541-252 MYA				Mesozoic 252-66 MYA		Cenozoic 66-0 MYA	

EUPARKERIA
YOO-par-KER-ee-a

MEANING: "Parker's good animal"
PERIOD: Middle Triassic
LOCALITY: South Africa
LENGTH: 1.6-3.2 ft
WEIGHT: 4.4-8.8 lbs
DIET: Carnivore

This little archosaur relative scurried around the undergrowth of southern Africa around 240 million years ago. Although it might have been capable of moving on its hind legs, it probably spent most of its time on all fours, and the arrangement of its anklebones suggests a gait similar to the crocodilian "high walk."

INNER EAR STRUCTURE
Euparkeria's inner ear was advanced compared to more primitive reptiles. It could hear a wider range of sounds, which was useful for detecting both prey and would-be predators. Reconstruction of parts of the brain that affect body movements show that it was an upright, agile little predator.

Listening out for rustling sounds in the undergrowth, this *Euparkeria* needed to be alert for both predators and potential meals.

NIGHT HUNTER
Some fossils of *Euparkeria* contain a sclerotic ring within the eye socket. This ring is made up of tiny bones and helps support the eyeball. The relative size of the sclerotic ring matches known species that are active at night, so *Euparkeria* may have been most active during low light conditions.

| Devonian 419-359 MYA | Carboniferous 359-299 MYA | Permian 299-252 MYA | Triassic 252-201 MYA | Jurassic 201-145 MYA | Cretaceous 145-66 MYA | Paleogene 66-23 MYA | Neogene 23-3 MYA | 49 |

Paleozoic 541-252 MYA | Mesozoic 252-66 MYA | Cenozoic 66-0 MYA

JURASSIC ERA

201–145 million years ago

Just over 200 million years ago, the supercontinent Pangaea split into two new landmasses—Laurasia to the north and Gondwana to the south—creating extensive new habitats for organisms to exploit. This split provided more coastlines, and therefore more rain, meaning the climate was wetter than the Triassic. It was still warm, and plants flourished in the new conditions.

Now free from competitors after the mass extinction at the end of the Triassic, dinosaurs began evolving into an amazing array of forms. Some, like the sauropods, became truly gigantic, while others such as the stegosaurs experimented with new forms of display and defense. The theropods were the top predators, stalking the rich landscapes for potential meals. Mammals had evolved, but they remained in the shadow of the dinosaurs, with some leading nocturnal lifestyles to avoid being eaten.

In the air, the pterosaurs were joined by a new group of flying vertebrates: the birds. Birds first evolved in the Jurassic from a lineage of feathered theropods, although many of their early representatives still possessed "typical" dinosaur traits such as teeth and a bony tail. The seas were still the dominion of the various reptile groups such as the ichthyosaurs, but marine invertebrates such as ammonites were still doing well.

DILOPHOSAURUS
Die-LOF-oh-sor-us

The double crest lining its snout was too fragile to be used as a weapon. It was probably a display to attract mates.

MEANING: "Two-crested lizard"
PERIOD: Early Jurassic
LOCALITY: North America
LENGTH: 22 ft
WEIGHT: 600-800 lbs
DIET: Carnivore

With its instantly recognizable double crest and notched snout, *Dilophosaurus* was a large yet primitive theropod dinosaur. Stalking the Early Jurassic floodplains, it probably fed on prey smaller than itself.

WEAK BITER

Dilophosaurus probably had a relatively weak bite, especially at the back of its jaws. However, the tip of its snout was expanded, and its lower jaws were tightly joined together at the front, making it likely that it captured prey using the front of its mouth.

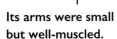

Its arms were small but well-muscled.

BROKEN BONES

The fossils of one *Dilophosaurus* tell a painful story. The arms and shoulder girdle show evidence of various diseases and healed injuries, which would have made hunting difficult. However, the creature survived for a long while, suggesting either that it managed to go without food for extended periods of time, or that its arms were not necessary for catching prey.

	Devonian 419-359 MYA	Carboniferous 359-299 MYA	Permian 299-252 MYA	Triassic 252-201 MYA	Jurassic 201-145 MYA	Cretaceous 145-66 MYA	Paleogene 66-23 MYA	Neogene 23-3 MYA
	Paleozoic 541-252 MYA				**Mesozoic** 252-66 MYA		**Cenozoic** 66-0 MYA	

SCELIDOSAURUS

SKEL-i-do-SOR-us

MEANING: "Limb lizard"
PERIOD: Early Jurassic
LOCALITY: United Kingdom
LENGTH: 13 ft
WEIGHT: 550-700 lbs
DIET: Herbivore

This early thyreophoran herbivore was closely related to the giant stegosaurs and ankylosaurs. Like its later relatives, it was well armored, with rows of osteoderms lining its neck, back, and tail. The skeleton of a *Scelidosaurus* was one of the most complete ever found in the British Isles.

PLANT POWER

Scelidosaurus probably ate ferns and young conifers, nipping off low-lying vegetation and crushing it with a simple up-and-down motion of its jaws. A plant-based diet may have pushed thyreophorans (and other ornithischians) to a four-legged lifestyle, as digesting plants requires a long gut.

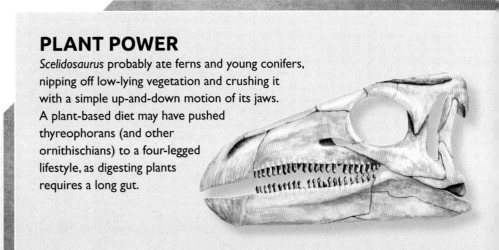

WATERY GRAVE

The best-preserved *Scelidosaurus* skeleton was found in marine deposits, but this doesn't mean it lived in the ocean. It's more likely that it died near a river before being washed out to sea with the tide, sinking to the seafloor and being buried in soft mud. This mud was the reason its skeleton was so well preserved.

Scelidosaurus probably had a beak that helped it nip off vegetation.

Devonian	Carboniferous	Permian	Triassic	Jurassic	Cretaceous	Paleogene	Neogene
419-359 MYA	359-299 MYA	299-252 MYA	252-201 MYA	201-145 MYA	145-66 MYA	66-23 MYA	23-3 MYA
Paleozoic 541-252 MYA				Mesozoic 252-66 MYA		Cenozoic 66-0 MYA	

KULINDADROMEUS

KOO-lin-dah-DROH-mee-us

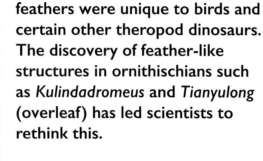

MEANING: "Kulinda runner"
PERIOD: Middle Jurassic
LOCALITY: Russia
LENGTH: 4.9 ft
WEIGHT: 33 lbs
DIET: Herbivore

Until recently it was thought that feathers were unique to birds and certain other theropod dinosaurs. The discovery of feather-like structures in ornithischians such as *Kulindadromeus* and *Tianyulong* (overleaf) has led scientists to rethink this.

The flattened skull of *Kulindadromeus* shows teeth adapted for a plant based diet.

The small jaws of *Kulindadromeus* were adapted for feeding on undergrowth.

KULINDADROMEUS
This small herbivore grew three types of feather-like structures. Simple filaments covered its head and body; longer, grouped filaments grew on its upper arms and legs; and unique, ribbon-shaped structures made up of around ten individual filaments covered the tops of its shins. The rest of its body was scaled.

	Devonian 419-359 MYA	Carboniferous 359-299 MYA	Permian 299-252 MYA	Triassic 252-201 MYA	Jurassic 201-145 MYA	Cretaceous 145-66 MYA	Paleogene 66-23 MYA	Neogene 23-3 MYA
	Paleozoic 541-252 MYA				Mesozoic 252-66 MYA		Cenozoic 66-0 MYA	

TIANYULONG

Tee-AN-yu-LONG

MEANING: "Tianyu dragon"
PERIOD: Late Jurassic
LOCALITY: China
LENGTH: 2.2 ft
WEIGHT: 15 lbs
DIET: Herbivore/ Omnivore

Tianyulong was a small, Late Jurassic ornithischian that scampered around the humid, subtropical forests of what would become China. A series of filaments sprouted from its neck, back and hips, some reaching 2 inches long. This suggests that feathers appeared much earlier in the history of life than was once thought.

UNRAVELLING DNA

Analysis of living vertebrates shows that the genetic instructions for making feathers had evolved at least 250 million years ago. This is backed by fossil evidence that suggests some sort of feathers may have been present in the common ancestor of both dinosaurs and pterosaurs. Feathers first evolved as simple filaments whose primary purpose may have been to help keep these ancient reptiles warm.

TIANYULONG

Tianyulong was a heterodontosaurid, a kind of primitive ornithischian known for their varied teeth. The small, canine-like teeth at the front of its jaws, along with chisel-shaped teeth lining the back, gave *Tianyulong* the tools to process many different foods. Whether its diet was wholly plant-based, or included some meat, is unknown.

Devonian 419-359 MYA	Carboniferous 359-299 MYA	Permian 299-252 MYA	Triassic 252-201 MYA	Jurassic 201-145 MYA	Cretaceous 145-66 MYA	Paleogene 66-23 MYA	Neogene 23-3 MYA
Paleozoic 541-252 MYA			Mesozoic 252-66 MYA			Cenozoic 66-0 MYA	

LEEDSICHTHYS

LEEDS-ik-THIS

MEANING: "Leeds' fish"
PERIOD: Middle Jurassic
LOCALITY: Europe, Chile
LENGTH: 36-54 ft
WEIGHT: 49 tons
DIET: Small invertebrates

Leedsichthys belongs to a group of suspension-feeders (animals that feed on particles suspended in water) that cruised the Jurassic and Cretaceous seas, probably in perpetual search of shoals of small crustaceans to fuel their bulk. When fossils were first found, scientists believed it grew to an astonishing 98 ft long. However, recent studies based on greater evidence have halved that figure.

These two giants cruise at the ocean's surface in search for food. It took them 40 years to reach their large size.

TOOTHLESS GIANT

Like many suspension feeders, *Leedsichthys* completely lacked teeth. Instead, it possessed highly developed gill rakers (little projections on the surface of the gill arches). As water passed over them, these sieved out tiny invertebrates, which the fish then swallowed.

SHARED ANATOMY

Leedsichthys's large body size, jaw modifications, and lack of teeth made it similar to modern filter feeders, such as whale sharks and baleen whales. This is another example of convergent evolution, where distantly related forms evolve similar traits in order to exploit a similar lifestyle.

Curved, elongated pectoral fins probably had a role in steering as *Leedsichthys*'s large tail propelled it through the water.

Devonian 419-359 MYA	Carboniferous 359-299 MYA	Permian 299-252 MYA	Triassic 252-201 MYA	Jurassic 201-145 MYA	Cretaceous 145-66 MYA	Paleogene 66-23 MYA	Neogene 23-3 MYA
Paleozoic 541-252 MYA			Mesozoic 252-66 MYA			Cenozoic 66-0 MYA	

GUANLONG

GWAN-LONG

MEANING: "Crown dragon"
PERIOD: Late Jurassic
LOCALITY: China
LENGTH: 9.8 ft
WEIGHT: 220 lbs
DIET: Carnivore

This primitive tyrannosaur, which was relatively small compared to its later cousins, is known from two fossils that were found buried in a wetland environment. Like *Dilong*, another early Chinese tyrannosaur that was preserved with evidence of soft tissue, it was probably covered in simple feathers. It sported a showy crest along its snout.

FLASHY CREST

Guanlong's thin crest was filled with air spaces, and was too delicate to be used during fights. The younger fossilized specimen had a smaller crest than the adult one, suggesting that it might have been used to attract mates, similar to the crests of many modern animals today.

Guanlong's narrow jaws meant it probably didn't have a strong bite, and targeted small prey.

Slinking through the undergrowth, this adult *Guanlong* is on the prowl.

Although there is no direct evidence that *Guanlong* had feathers, this seems likely based on fossils of its close relatives.

Three long fingers made up *Guanlong*'s hand. They were perhaps used for grabbing or spearing prey.

Devonian 419-359 MYA	Carboniferous 359-299 MYA	Permian 299-252 MYA	Triassic 252-201 MYA	Jurassic 201-145 MYA	Cretaceous 145-66 MYA	Paleogene 66-23 MYA	Neogene 23-3 MYA
Paleozoic 541-252 MYA			Mesozoic 252-66 MYA			Cenozoic 66-0 MYA	

MARINE REPTILES

Reptiles were much more diverse in the Mesozoic seas than they are today, and several different groups evolved to exploit the marine environment. Some reached gigantic proportions, becoming top predators in the process. Four major groups developed following the Triassic-Jurassic extinction: the ichthyosaurs, the plesiosaurs, the sea turtles, and the mosasaurs. In addition, some surviving pseudosuchians also became relatively successful.

INVASION OF THE SEAS

All marine reptiles descended from various terrestrial ancestors. However, returning to an aquatic environment is particularly challenging for an ectothermic (cold-blooded) reptile, as heat is lost more quickly in water than in air. Fortunately, compared to endotherms (the so called "warm-blooded" animals, like us mammals), reptiles are better at handling cooler temperatures, and they use energy much more efficiently. In addition, they can survive for longer periods without oxygen than equally sized mammals, meaning that their ancestors were well adapted for conquering the Early Triassic seas.

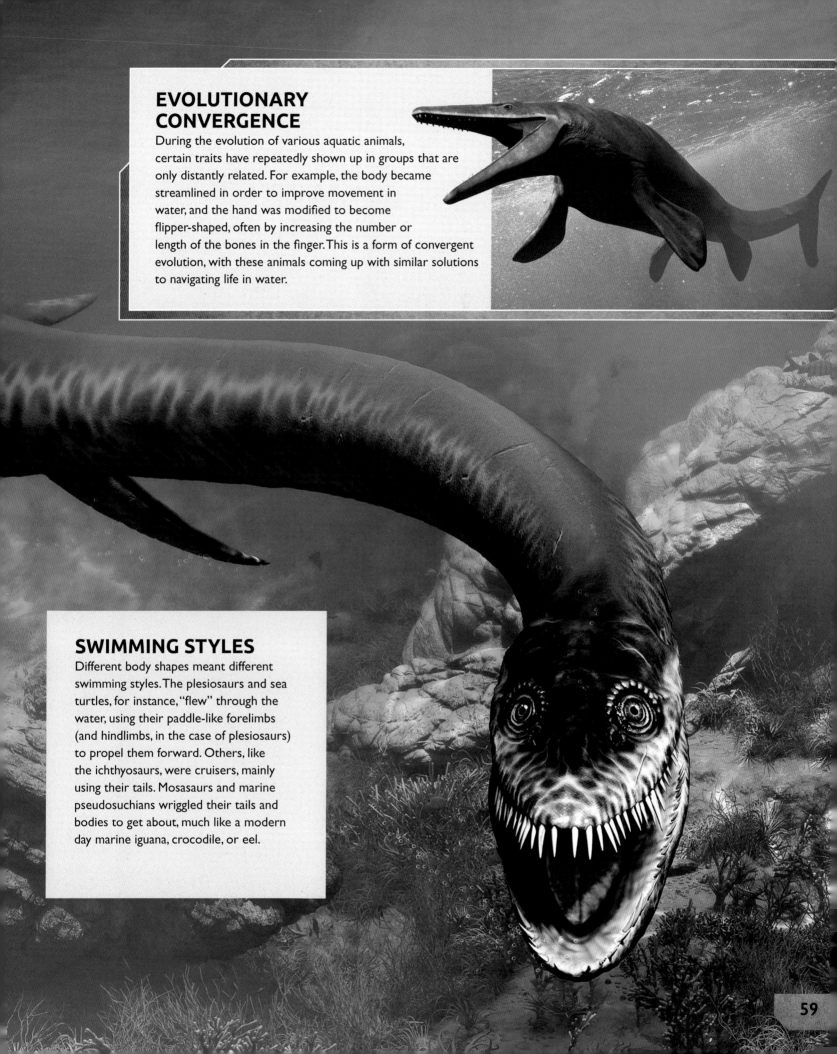

EVOLUTIONARY CONVERGENCE

During the evolution of various aquatic animals, certain traits have repeatedly shown up in groups that are only distantly related. For example, the body became streamlined in order to improve movement in water, and the hand was modified to become flipper-shaped, often by increasing the number or length of the bones in the finger. This is a form of convergent evolution, with these animals coming up with similar solutions to navigating life in water.

SWIMMING STYLES

Different body shapes meant different swimming styles. The plesiosaurs and sea turtles, for instance, "flew" through the water, using their paddle-like forelimbs (and hindlimbs, in the case of plesiosaurs) to propel them forward. Others, like the ichthyosaurs, were cruisers, mainly using their tails. Mosasaurs and marine pseudosuchians wriggled their tails and bodies to get about, much like a modern day marine iguana, crocodile, or eel.

PLESIOSAURS

PLES-i-oh-SORS

Interlocking teeth
helped snap up fish.

The first Triassic plesiosaur was
only discovered in 2017. Until
then, the group appeared to
have evolved "out of nowhere"
during the Early Jurassic. These
were among the most successful
vertebrates in the history of life
on Earth, navigating the seas
right up until the end of the
Cretaceous, 66 million years ago.
Their diet ranged from small fish
and invertebrates to other marine
reptiles, depending on the species.

Using all four flippers to push
itself through the water, this
plesiosaur is scanning the
ocean for prey.

WARM-BLOODED?

Recent studies have suggested that plesiosaurs grew quickly, with juveniles putting on a lot of mass in their first year. They may even have been endothermic, generating heat internally like mammals. This ability may have contributed to their success, allowing them to explore a wider range of habitats. Other evidence, such as fossils from Australia and Antarctica found in deposits showing evidence for extreme cold-water temperatures, supports this idea.

EXTREME BODY SHAPES

Plesiosaurs can be divided into two basic body shapes. The first were the long-necked forms, with some later species boasting 19-inch-long skulls attached to 23-ft-long necks. These probably ate smaller prey. The other group, also known as the pliosaurs, were the opposite. They had smaller necks topped by huge 6.5-ft-long skulls that made them some of the top predators in the Mesozoic seas.

Plesiosaurs may have had a small tail fluke.

POWERFUL FLIPPERS

A plesiosaur's limbs were heavily modified in order to propel its body through the water. Its front and back flippers were all large and rigid, while its wrist and anklebones were big and tightly packed together. Meanwhile, its elbow and knee joints were inflexible, and its finger bones increased in number to create a paddle-like limb. In its chest and hips, the bones became huge in order to provide attachment points for powerful muscles.

ICHTHYOSAURS

IK-thee-o-SORS

The ichthyosaurs appeared before the plesiosaurs, not long into the Triassic. They were another extremely successful, long-lived group of marine reptiles, thriving until 90 million years ago. The early forms included some of the largest marine reptiles ever, reaching lengths of over 65 ft. Later species are known for their fish-shaped anatomy.

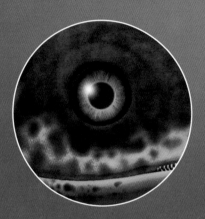

WHAT BIG EYES YOU HAVE...

Ichthyosaurs had famously huge eyes. *Temnodontosaurus*' were around 10 inches in diameter, while *Ophthalmosaurus* had the largest eyes relative to body size of any vertebrate. It is thought these giant eyes were used to track fast-moving prey, or helped them see in the ocean depths where they hunted. However, like all reptiles, they had to come up to breathe.

COLOR PATTERNS

Unusually, palaeontologists have been able to recreate the color patterns of some ichthyosaurs after preserved pigments were discovered with some fossilized skeletons. Some ichthyosaurs show a coloration pattern known as countershading, where the top half is darker than the bottom. These help camouflage the animal when viewed from above and below, a useful trait in the dangerous Mesozoic seas.

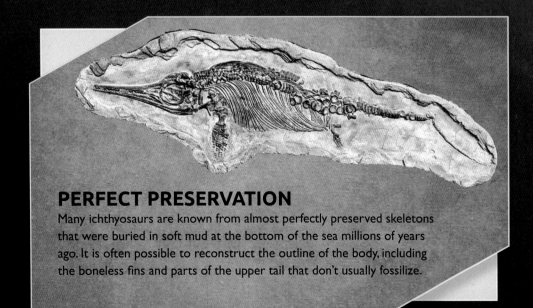

PERFECT PRESERVATION

Many ichthyosaurs are known from almost perfectly preserved skeletons that were buried in soft mud at the bottom of the sea millions of years ago. It is often possible to reconstruct the outline of the body, including the boneless fins and parts of the upper tail that don't usually fossilize.

SKIN DEEP

Thanks to the wonderful preservation of some ichthyosaur fossils, palaeontologists have been able to examine their soft tissues in incredible detail. Their skin was scaleless and flexible, and sat on top of a layer of fatty blubber. This suggests they had evolved the ability to generate internal heat, and they used the blubber to keep warm, perhaps when they were diving deep after prey.

A group of ichthyosaurs prepares to dive in search of food.

CROCODYLOMORPHS
CROC-oh-DIE-lo-MORFS

Crocodylomorphs, the category that includes modern crocodilians and their extinct relatives, were the only pseudosuchian survivors of the Triassic-Jurassic mass extinction. Those that survived into the Jurassic developed into a whole range of different body shapes. One group in particular became increasingly tied to water. These were the the thalattosuchia, or "ocean crocodiles."

THALATTOSUCHIA FAMILY TREE

The ocean crocodiles can be split into two groups: the semi-aquatic teleosaurids, which could crawl out onto land; and the fully aquatic metriorhynchids, which possessed tail fins, and paddle-like hands and feet. They may also have had special glands to help flush out the salt that built up in their bodies.

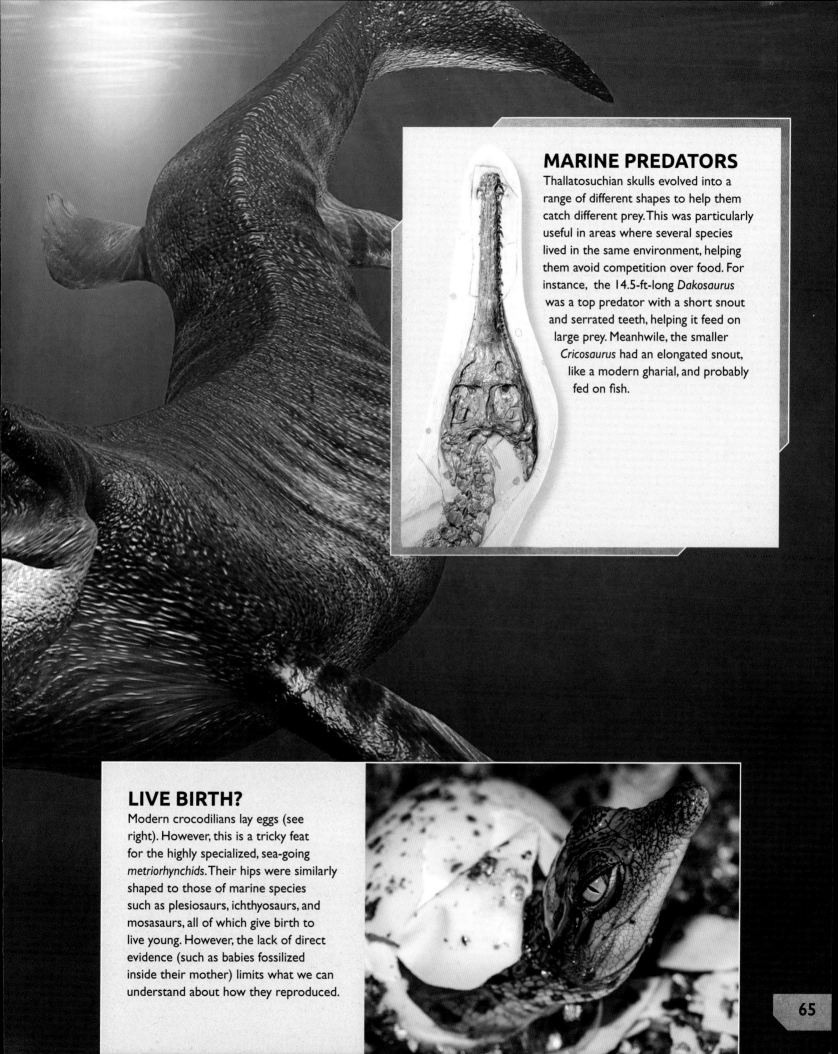

MARINE PREDATORS

Thallatosuchian skulls evolved into a range of different shapes to help them catch different prey. This was particularly useful in areas where several species lived in the same environment, helping them avoid competition over food. For instance, the 14.5-ft-long *Dakosaurus* was a top predator with a short snout and serrated teeth, helping it feed on large prey. Meanwhile, the smaller *Cricosaurus* had an elongated snout, like a modern gharial, and probably fed on fish.

LIVE BIRTH?

Modern crocodilians lay eggs (see right). However, this is a tricky feat for the highly specialized, sea-going *metriorhynchids*. Their hips were similarly shaped to those of marine species such as plesiosaurs, ichthyosaurs, and mosasaurs, all of which give birth to live young. However, the lack of direct evidence (such as babies fossilized inside their mother) limits what we can understand about how they reproduced.

AMMONITES

AM-on-EYE-ts

They might look like snails, but these hugely successful marine invertebrates are actually cephalopods, more closely related to squid and octopuses. They first evolved in the Devonian, producing a huge variety of shapes and sizes up until their eventual extinction at the end of the Cretaceous.

Its hard shell protected the soft internal structures of the ammonite.

MISSING SOFT TISSUES

Millions of fossilized ammonites have been found around the world, but exactly what soft tissues their shells contained is still unknown. They probably had tentacles to capture small prey, while some may have evolved filter feeding methods as well.

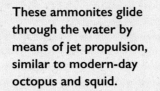

These ammonites glide through the water by means of jet propulsion, similar to modern-day octopus and squid.

AMMONITE SHELL

The shell probably had multiple functions. It served as a buoyancy device, as the air-filled compartments helped the cephalopod move up and down the water column. Spikes on the surface of some shells may have acted as protection against hungry marine predators, or helped attract a mate.

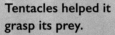

Tentacles helped it grasp its prey.

THE PALAEONTOLOGIST'S FRIEND

Ammonites evolved quickly and are easy to find all over the world. This makes them useful for figuring out the age of marine sediments, as the pattern on an ammonite shell tells paleontologists what species it belonged to. Ammonites evolved rapidly, with new species replacing older ones every few hundred thousand years—a blink of an eye in geological time—so scientists can use them to date rocks very precisely.

DIPLODOCUS
Dee-PLOD-oh-cus

MEANING: "Double beam"
PERIOD: Late Jurassic
LOCALITY: North America
LENGTH: 108 ft
WEIGHT: 11-13 tons
DIET: Herbivore

This long sauropod ambled around the floodplains of Late Jurassic North America on a never-ending search for vegetation. It was one of several giant sauropods navigating their way through this ecosystem, and it likely had to modify its lifestyle to avoid direct competition for food and space.

HOLLOW BONES

The neck, back, and some tail bones of sauropods like *Diplodocus* were filled with air spaces. These air sacs, which are little extensions of the lungs similar to those seen in modern birds, helped lighten the skeleton. Some estimates suggest *Diplodocus* would have weighed another 1.6 tons had its bones been solid!

This adult *Diplodocus* roams the semi-arid plains of North America on an almost continuous quest for food.

This *Diplodocus* leg bone was excavated in Wyoming, USA in 1898.

TEETH
The simple teeth were located at the front of the jaw.

FEEDING RANGE
The way *Diplodocus* held its neck would have affected what kind of food it could eat. Some experts think it kept its neck horizontal, meaning the sauropod could only eat low-lying plants. More recent reconstructions show that the head was probably held high. *Diplodocus* may have even been able to rear up on its hind legs, giving it access to food both high and low.

HEAD ANATOMY
Diplodocus' small, narrow head had long, peg-like teeth at the front of the jaws. Computer models of the skull have shown that its most likely method of feeding was either to strip branches of their leaves, or to precisely nip off vegetation from trees, as these put the least stress on the skull. Unlike modern mammalian herbivores, *Diplodocus* did not chew its food, but just swallowed it whole.

JAWS
Dipolodocus ate around 72 lbs of ferns every day.

NECK
The long neck probably evolved to help the animal reach for leaves to eat, but may also have played a small role in heat loss.

WATCH IT NOW
View this page in the app to see Diplodocus in motion.

SCAN THIS PAGE

CERATOSAURUS

seh-RAT-o-SOR-us

MEANING: "Horn lizard"
PERIOD: Late Jurassic
LOCALITY: Europe, North America
LENGTH: 16-22 ft
WEIGHT: 1,543 lbs
DIET: Carnivore

Ceratosaurus was one of the smaller "large" theropods of the Late Jurassic. Its distinctive crest and the small horns above its eyes gave it a fearsome appearance. Fossils have been found in both Europe and North America, suggesting that an ancient land bridge connected the two continents around 150 million years ago.

The long tail provided balance as the predator stalked around on two legs.

CRESTED SKULL

When *Ceratosaurus* was first discovered in the late 19th Century, palaeontologists thought the 6 inch horn on its snout was used as a weapon against predators and prey. We now think it could also have been used for fights with other *Ceratosaurus* over mates, or that it wasn't used for fighting at all, but rather for display. The fact that younger *Ceratosaurus* had smaller horns might be significant, as this is what would happen if they were used to attract mates as the animal matured.

The horns were probably covered in a tough keratin sheath.

FIERCE COMPETITION

Ceratosaurus shared environments with at least two other big predators: the more common *Allosaurus*, and the rare *Torvosaurus*. To avoid clashing over resources, these dinosaurs probably used different hunting styles. The teeth of *Ceratosaurus* were relatively long, perhaps giving it a different biting style to its competitors, and it was smaller in size so may have tackled smaller prey. Some researchers have even suggested it lived nearer to water than the other two carnivores, perhaps feeding on crocodiles and lungfish as well as land prey.

TINY ARMS

Ceratosaurus gives its name to the ceratosaurs, theropods which often had famously puny arms. In *Ceratosaurus*, the bones were shortened but probably still had some grasping function, but the claws were much smaller than those of other predators of the time. This shrinking of the forelimb happened throughout the ceratosaur group, and suggests that biting was becoming their main means of catching prey.

Using its relatively well-developed sense of smell, this *Ceratosaurus* has detected an intruder on its territory.

PTEROSAURS

TEH-roh-sors

These winged reptiles were the first vertebrates to evolve powered flight—another archosaur success story. Pterosaurs were more closely related to dinosaurs than pseudosuchians. After they evolved in the Triassic, they rapidly developed during the Jurassic, producing lots of diverse species all the way until the mass extinction at the end of the Cretaceous.

LIGHTWEIGHT SKELETON

Although over 130 species of pterosaur are known today, there are probably plenty more undiscovered. The extreme fragility of their skeletons meant that they didn't often get fossilized. Their bones were very thin, but were supported internally by bony struts, making them extremely strong. This helped them deal with the stresses of flight.

WING MEMBRANE

In pterosaurs, the arms evolved into wings, with the membrane attached to an extremely elongated fourth finger. A unique bone also jutted out from the wrist, to help connect the membrane to the shoulder. Pterosaurs could actually alter the shape of their wings thanks to a thin layer of muscle and nerves inside the membrane. This helped them become masters of the air.

FUZZY COAT

Pterosaurs were covered in small hairlike structures called pycnofibres. These were made of the same materials as theropod feathers, so theropods evolved from the same ancestor. The pycnofibres probably worked as insulation, as evidence has suggested these animals were warm-blooded and needed to retain heat.

STEGOSAURUS
STEG-o-SOR-us

MEANING: "Roof lizard"
PERIOD: Late Jurassic
LOCALITY: North America, Europe
LENGTH: 16-29 ft
WEIGHT: 1.7-8.1 tons
DIET: Herbivore

SCAN THIS PAGE

Stegosaurus is one of the most iconic dinosaurs of the Late Jurassic, although it is best known for the unflattering fact of having a tiny brain relative to its body size. Its skeletons have been found in both North America and Western Europe. In spite of its fearsome back plates and spiked tail, it was a herbivore, probably eating low-growing plants like ferns and shrubs.

ARMORED HERBIVORE

Different stegosaurs often had different arrangements of the plates and spikes on their body. Large, flat dorsal plates lined *Stegosaurus'* back and upper tail, and several skeletons of the predator *Allosaurus* have been found showing puncture marks that fit *Stegosaurus* spikes. Some skeletons have even been found with broken spikes that had started to heal. The plates probably weren't used in defense, as they were no good for protecting the animal's exposed flanks, but may have been used in some form of display.

BIG GUT

The hip region of *Stegosaurus* was extremely wide. This provided extra space for the long gut it housed, important for herbivores as plant material is tough to digest and it takes a long time to extract nutrients from it.

HEAD
Stegosaurs had sharp beaks that they used to slice into plants.

SPIKED TAIL
The tail was flexible and could be swung with some force.

LEGS
Stegosaurus had three toes on its hind limb.

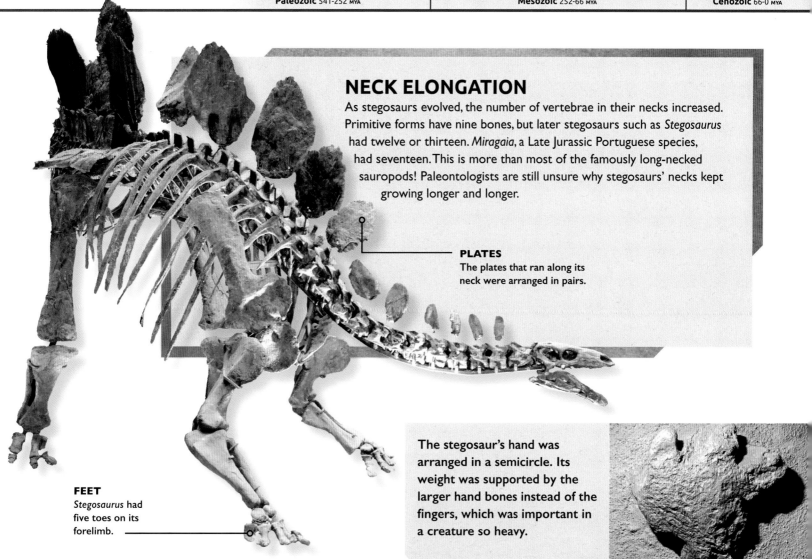

NECK ELONGATION

As stegosaurs evolved, the number of vertebrae in their necks increased. Primitive forms have nine bones, but later stegosaurs such as *Stegosaurus* had twelve or thirteen. *Miragaia*, a Late Jurassic Portuguese species, had seventeen. This is more than most of the famously long-necked sauropods! Paleontologists are still unsure why stegosaurs' necks kept growing longer and longer.

PLATES
The plates that ran along its neck were arranged in pairs.

FEET
Stegosaurus had five toes on its forelimb.

The stegosaur's hand was arranged in a semicircle. Its weight was supported by the larger hand bones instead of the fingers, which was important in a creature so heavy.

SCAN THIS PAGE

WATCH IT NOW
View this page in the app to see Stegosaurus in motion.

ALLOSAURUS

AL-oh-SOR-us

MEANING: "Different lizard"
PERIOD: Late Jurassic
LOCALITY: Europe, North America
LENGTH: 31 ft
WEIGHT: 1.4–1.9 tons
DIET: Carnivore

The fearsome *Allosaurus* was built on the traditional theropod body plan: a bipedal stance, powerful arms and jaws lined with serrated teeth. It was the most common large predator in some Late Jurassic ecosystems, and paleontologists have found several well-preserved specimens, making it one of the better-studied dinosaurs.

GROWTH SPURTS

Like other large theropods, *Allosaurus* grew quickly. Some of the youngest specimens, which are thought to be about three years old, weigh around 59 lbs. At around 15 years of age, teenage *Allosaurus* really packed on the pounds, with a maximum growth rate of 326 lbs per year. This rate slowed as it got older, with the oldest individuals likely dying at around 28 years old. Large carnivorous dinosaurs seldom grew this old, as being a predator is a dangerous lifestyle.

PICKY EATER

Allosaurus' neck muscles helped it feed off carcasses in a similar way to modern falcons or kestrels. It pinned its meal to the ground then rapidly pulled its neck up, stripping the flesh from the bone.

Allosaurus' head crest may have been used for display.

UNUSUAL ATTACK

Allosaurus probably tackled mid-sized prey, like young herbivores or the small ornithopod *Camptosaurus*. Its skull is very well adapted to resisting stress, and it could open its mouth extremely wide. Its actual bite force was weak, however. This combination of traits may have meant it used its upper jaw like a hatchet, delivering long, slashing wounds with its teeth.

Allosaurus teeth were relatively short, at around 1 or 2 inches long.

JURASSIC GIANT?

Some other fossils found near *Allosaurus* bones belonged to animals that might have reached over 39 ft in length. However, scientists aren't sure whether these were giant *Allosaurus*, or completely different theropods.

SCAN THIS PAGE

ARCHAEOPTERYX
AR-kee-OP-tuh-rix

MEANING: "Old wing"
PERIOD: Late Jurassic
LOCALITY: Europe
LENGTH: 1.6 ft
WEIGHT: 2.2 lbs
DIET: Insectivore

SCAN THIS PAGE

Archaeopteryx is seen as "the first bird." With a combination of modern avian and ancient reptilian traits, it has been vital to scientists studying the complex family history linking birds to theropod dinosaurs. Several exquisitely preserved specimens found in Germany have helped researchers take a really detailed look at this amazing creature.

FIRST FLIGHT

Archeopteryx is the most famous prehistoric flier, but X-ray analysis shows that the shape and structure of its wing bones resembled those of modern-day quails and pheasants, meaning it could probably only take to the air in short bursts. However, the way it flapped its wings was unlike anything alive today, and is still under study.

TEETH
Its teeth were smooth, not serrated like those of other theropods.

REPTILIAN TRAITS

While it possessed some characteristics of modern birds, *Archaeopteryx* still retained reptilian traits. Its pointed teeth helped it capture small reptiles and insects. It even possessed the famous, elevated "killer claw" of its dinosaur cousins the maniraptorans, which might have played a role in pinning prey to the ground.

CLAWS
Its hand still had clawed fingers, like reptiles.

SCAN THIS PAGE

WATCH IT NOW
View this page in the app to see Archaeopteryx in motion.

FEATHERS
The feathers on its wings were similar to those of modern birds, allowing limited flight.

TAIL
Archeopteryx's tail provided balance when it walked on the ground.

STUNNING PRESERVATION

Archaeopteryx scampered around what would become modern-day Germany. The forests where it lived bordered very salty, oxygen-poor lagoons, and some creatures fell into the water and drowned. The conditions meant that bacteria could not easily break down soft tissues, so they were gently buried, preserving imprints of the wing and tail feathers as well as bones.

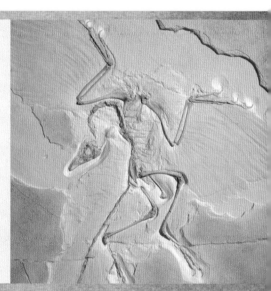

PLUMAGE COLORS

Scientists have been able to identify fossilized pigments in a feather thought to have come from *Archaeopteryx*. These pigments were similarly shaped to those found in modern animals that have black coloration, so *Archaeopteryx* probably had mostly black plumage. However, there is some debate as to whether the feather belonged to *Archaeopteryx* or to a completely different animal.

85

CRETACEOUS ERA

145–66 million years ago

Towards the end of the Mesozoic, our planet's landmasses split into continents and drifted into the positions they hold today. The climate was still generally warm, but Earth saw cooler periods from time to time, with some places even recording near-freezing temperatures during certain months.

A new type of vegetation evolved during this time: the flowering plants. They became a new food source for the herbivorous animals of the time. Dinosaurs remained the dominant terrestrial vertebrate, and several new groups appeared, including the horned ceratopsians. Birds continued to diversify, while pterosaurs grew larger and larger.

The end of the Cretaceous saw another devastating extinction event. An asteroid over 6 miles wide collided with the Earth in the Gulf of Mexico. Animals living near the impact were instantly vaporized, and tsunamis hundreds of miles tall crashed into ocean shores all around the world. The impact ejected billions of tons of fine particles and gases into the atmosphere, cooling temperatures for several years after. All the non-avian dinosaurs, the pterosaurs, and many of the marine reptile groups died out, but the birds, crocodilians, and mammals survived.

IGUANODON

i-GWAN-o-don

MEANING: "Iguana tooth"
PERIOD: Early Cretaceous
LOCALITY: Europe
LENGTH: 32-36 ft
WEIGHT: 2.7-4.4 tons
DIET: Herbivore

This huge, bulky ornithopod marched around Europe during the Early Cretaceous, using its tough beak to consume the lush vegetation in its habitat. Its thick lower jaw would have provided sturdy attachment points for powerful jaw muscles, helping it grind down its food with its broad, serrated teeth.

INITIAL DISCOVERY

The first fossils found of this herbivore were its teeth. When they were dug up in 1822, they puzzled the specialists of the time as no large, extinct plant-eating reptiles had yet been discovered. While some thought they looked a bit like the teeth of a pufferfish, others said they resembled those of the iguana—hence *Iguanodon's* name.

CLAWS
The fifth finger was more mobile than the rest, and might have been useful during foraging.

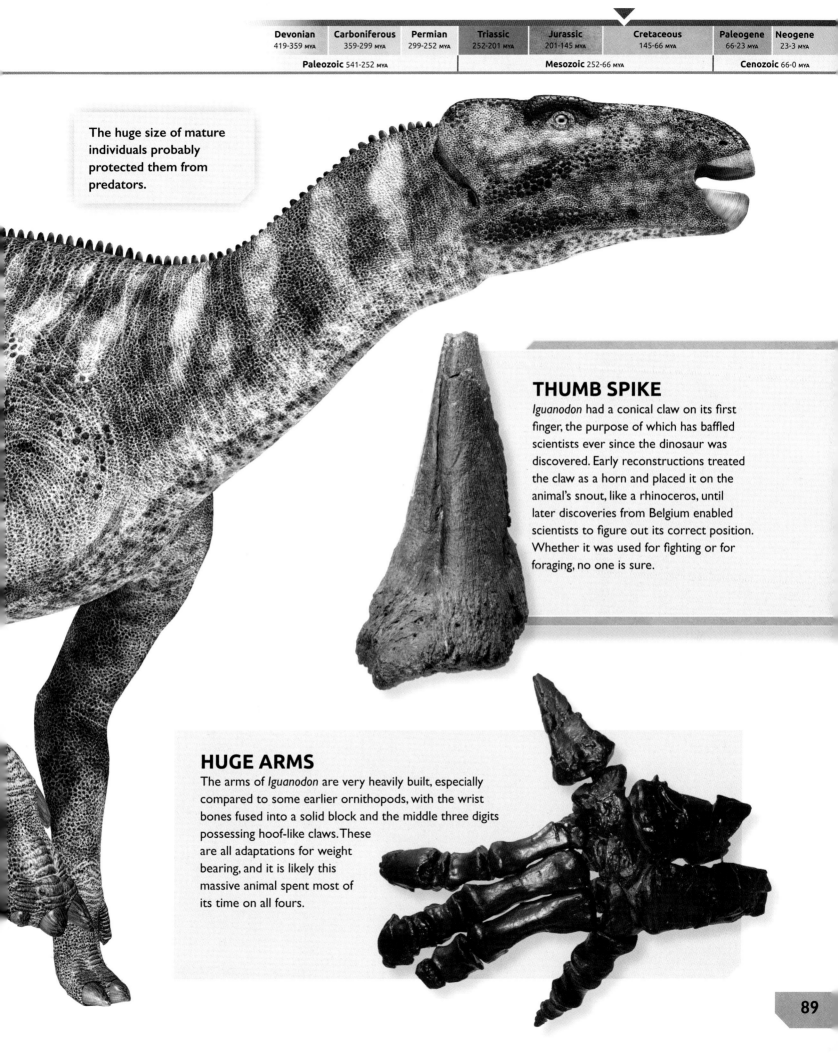

The huge size of mature individuals probably protected them from predators.

THUMB SPIKE

Iguanodon had a conical claw on its first finger, the purpose of which has baffled scientists ever since the dinosaur was discovered. Early reconstructions treated the claw as a horn and placed it on the animal's snout, like a rhinoceros, until later discoveries from Belgium enabled scientists to figure out its correct position. Whether it was used for fighting or for foraging, no one is sure.

HUGE ARMS

The arms of *Iguanodon* are very heavily built, especially compared to some earlier ornithopods, with the wrist bones fused into a solid block and the middle three digits possessing hoof-like claws. These are all adaptations for weight bearing, and it is likely this massive animal spent most of its time on all fours.

AMARGASAURUS
ah-MAHR-gah-SOR-us

MEANING: "La Amarga lizard"
PERIOD: Early Cretaceous
LOCALITY: Argentina
LENGTH: 29-32 ft
WEIGHT: 2.2 tons
DIET: Herbivore

Amargasaurus was bizarre in several ways. Most obvious were the huge spines that protruded from the vertebrae in its neck, but another feature made it stand out too: its "small" size. While a length of 32 ft and a weight of 2.2 tons might be seem hefty by modern standards (less than 10 percent of modern mammals grow above 1,100 lbs), *Amargasaurus* did not reach the large sizes typically seen in many other advanced sauropod groups.

A long neck and tail counterbalanced the body over the hips.

NECK SPINES

These grew up to 23 inches long and formed a double row that projected backward. Their narrow, delicate shape and position on top of *Amargasaurus*' neck might mean they were used to jab predators, as some modern horned herbivores like oryx do. However, their great length, along with the inflexibility of the animal's neck, suggests they had a display purpose instead. Interestingly, a recently discovered relative called *Bajadasaurus* had spines that projected forward!

SMALL GIANTS

Scientists aren't sure why *Amargasaurus* and its close relatives were smaller than most other advanced sauropods. It is likely that their short necks were adapted for browsing on low-growing vegetation. We have yet to find the front part of an *Amargasaurus* skull, but based on closely related forms, it was probably lined with simple teeth at the front.

Devonian 419-359 MYA	Carboniferous 359-299 MYA	Permian 299-252 MYA	Triassic 252-201 MYA	Jurassic 201-145 MYA	Cretaceous 145-66 MYA	Paleogene 66-23 MYA	Neogene 23-3 MYA
Paleozoic 541-252 MYA			Mesozoic 252-66 MYA			Cenozoic 66-0 MYA	

SARCOSUCHUS

SAR-co-SOO-kus

MEANING: "Flesh crocodile"
PERIOD: Early Cretaceous
LOCALITY: Africa, Brazil
LENGTH: 39 ft
WEIGHT: 8.8 tons
DIET: Carnivore

This giant predator patrolled the waterways of Cretaceous North Africa and Brazil. Twice as long as the largest crocodile alive today, it boasted a double row of giant, plate-like osteoderms covering the top of the neck, back and tail, and its skull featured an extremely long snout and distinctive overbite.

UNCERTAIN DIET

Given its large size, *Sarcosuchus* has often been portrayed as a dinosaur-killer, dragging the reptiles into the river as they came to drink. However, without the "death roll" (see the box to the right), how did it dismember large prey? It may have fed on large carcasses in some as-yet unknown way, and the chemical composition of its teeth suggests *Sarcosuchus* might have eaten a range of animals, including large fish and dinosaurs.

FEEDING STRATEGY

Sarcosuchus was not a crocodilian, but a more primitive cousin of modern-day species. Unlike most living types, however, *Sarcosuchus* was probably unable to manage the famous "death roll," the spinning maneuver that helps crocodilians rip chunks off prey. Its long snout would have been at risk of potentially bone-breaking stresses if it were to grab its prey and roll.

These ornithopods have disturbed a resting *Sarcosuchus*, who lurches away in disgust.

Devonian	Carboniferous	Permian	Triassic	Jurassic	Cretaceous	Paleogene	Neogene
419-359 MYA	359-299 MYA	299-252 MYA	252-201 MYA	201-145 MYA	145-66 MYA	66-23 MYA	23-3 MYA
Paleozoic 541-252 MYA				Mesozoic 252-66 MYA		Cenozoic 66-0 MYA	

91

BOREALOPELTA
BOH-ree-AH-low-PEL-tuh

MEANING: "Northern shield"
PERIOD: Early Cretaceous
LOCALITY: North America
LENGTH: 19 ft
WEIGHT: 1.4 tons
DIET: Herbivore

The wide, bulky *Borealopelta* was a typical ankylosaur, covered in thick spikes called osteoderms. This recent find is famous for its spectacular fossilization, which even preserved soft tissue and pigments, allowing palaeontologists to reconstruct the color of this tanklike herbivore.

HUES OF RED

The preserved pigments indicated that this stocky herbivore was reddish-brown on top and lighter in color below. This is a type of countershading, which is often used by prey species as a form of camouflage. However, in modern ecosystems, the larger a herbivore gets, the more uniform their coloration becomes, as they are not usually targeted by predators. As a result, the fact that *Borealopelta* possessed countershading despite being huge and armored suggests it was still on the menu for large theropods such as *Acrocanthosaurus*.

ARMOR OR DISPLAY?

Recent research suggests the big shoulder spines on the sides of *Borealopelta*, and perhaps some other ankylosaurs, did not evolve mainly for defense but to attract mates. These huge protrusions were probably a different color than the rest of the body, and might have helped the individual stand out.

Borealopelta's wide hips housed a long gut that helped extract a maximum amount of nutrients from its plant-based diet.

Devonian 419-359 MYA	Carboniferous 359-299 MYA	Permian 299-252 MYA	Triassic 252-201 MYA	Jurassic 201-145 MYA	Cretaceous 145-66 MYA	Paleogene 66-23 MYA	Neogene 23-3 MYA
Paleozoic 541-252 MYA			Mesozoic 252-66 MYA			Cenozoic 66-0 MYA	

CARCHARODONTOSAURUS

Kar-KA-ro-DON-toe-SOR-us

MEANING: "Shark-tooth lizard"
PERIOD: Early-Late Cretaceous
LOCALITY: Africa
LENGTH: 39-42 ft
WEIGHT: 5.5-6.6 tons
DIET: Carnivore

Cretaceous North Africa boasted a whole range of immense carnivorous theropods living together within the same ecosystem, and *Carcharodontosaurus* appears to have been the dominant land hunter. It takes its name from the flat, serrated, 3.5-inch-long teeth that look a bit like those of sharks. They were adapted for slicing through muscle.

The bone texture of *Carcharodontosaurus'* skull suggests its face was covered in tough skin.

BRAIN STUDIES

Reconstructions of the inside of *Carcharodontosaurus'* braincase show that its long brain had more in common with reptiles than birds. Its brain was relatively primitive for a therapod and similar to that of its cousin, *Allosaurus*.

RAW STRENGTH

Computer simulations show that *Carcharodontosaurus'* neck muscles could hypothetically lift around 934 lbs, while its jaws could clamp on to and hold an object weighing up to 1,128 lbs.

Its hand was made up of three fingers ending in large claws.

Devonian	Carboniferous	Permian	Triassic	Jurassic	Cretaceous	Paleogene	Neogene
419-359 MYA	359-299 MYA	299-252 MYA	252-201 MYA	201-145 MYA	145-66 MYA	66-23 MYA	23-3 MYA
Paleozoic 541-252 MYA			**Mesozoic** 252-66 MYA			**Cenozoic** 66-0 MYA	

SPINOSAURUS

SPINE-oh-SOR-us

MEANING: "Spine lizard"
PERIOD: Early-Late Cretaceous
LOCALITY: Africa
LENGTH: 49 ft
WEIGHT: 6.6-7.7 tons
DIET: Carnivore, piscivore

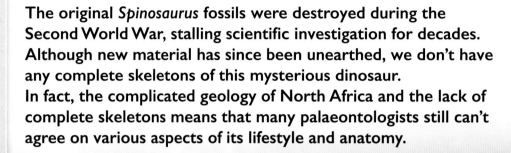

The original *Spinosaurus* fossils were destroyed during the Second World War, stalling scientific investigation for decades. Although new material has since been unearthed, we don't have any complete skeletons of this mysterious dinosaur.
In fact, the complicated geology of North Africa and the lack of complete skeletons means that many palaeontologists still can't agree on various aspects of its lifestyle and anatomy.

FLOATING THEROPOD

3D models of *Spinosaurus* have shown that it could not dive to catch prey, and was no better at swimming than any other theropod. As a result, it probably couldn't chase after prey in the water. Perhaps it hunted from the banks of the rivers that ran through its habitat.

Spinosaurus may have had shorter legs compared to its body than other theropods.

Spinosaurus' large dorsal sail may have been used for display.

SEMI-AQUATIC PREDATOR

Spinosaurus' long snout, its conical teeth, and the high placing of its nostrils suggest it could hunt in water. The teeth in particular show similarities with aquatic animals such as whales, crocodiles, and extinct marine reptiles.

Its nearly straight, conical teeth were well-suited for piercing prey.

FISH SPECIALIST?

Due to its crocodile-like appearance, *Spinosaurus* is often shown eating fish. Digested fish scales were found in the ribcage of its cousin *Baryonyx*. However, spinosaurids probably ate a variety of prey. One spinosaurid tooth was found embedded in the vertebrae of a pterosaur, while the bones of a young *Iguanodon* were found along with the fish scales inside the *Baryonyx* specimen. They probably had a generalized diet, and this helped them secure enough food in spite of competition from other large therapods.

ARGENTINOSAURUS

Ahr-jen-TEEN-o-SOR-us

MEANING: "Argentine lizard"
PERIOD: Late Cretaceous
LOCALITY: South America
LENGTH: 114 ft
WEIGHT: 88 tons
DIET: Herbivore

Quite possibly the largest terrestrial animal known to science, *Argentinosaurus* slowly shifted its huge frame around in search of up to 507 lbs of food per day. Like many giant sauropods, however, it is only known from several bones, including a giant thighbone measuring 8.2 ft in length.

The intimidating size of an adult *Argentinosaurus* suggests it was probably safe from almost any predator.

MISSING HEAD

We only have complete skulls of four of the 60 or so titanosaurs known. The delicate bones of the head fossilized less well than the huge leg bones, and for *Argentinosaurus* we have no skull material at all. This forces scientists to reconstruct its skull based on closely related species.

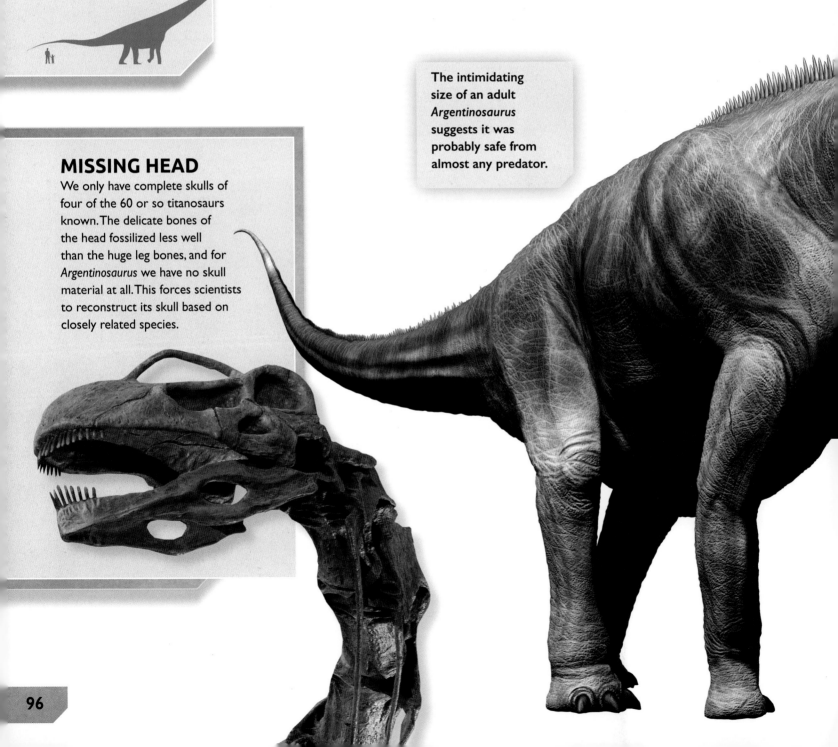

Argnetinosaurus likely had simple teeth. This means it didn't waste energy on chewing, allowing it to concentrate on simply eating more food.

GROUP NESTING

Even the largest dinosaurs started off small, hatching from eggs no bigger than a football. A famous nesting site in Argentina, created by a younger cousin of *Argentinosaurus*, shows a glimpse of how these titanosaurs reproduced. Four hundred simple nests were scratched out of the ground near a river, 6.5-9.8 ft apart, where around 30 eggs were laid per clutch. These titanosaurs returned to the same site often, and the preservation is so good that even the skin of unhatched embryos can be found. Sauropods probably did not care for their young, so the babies had to fend for themselves as soon as they hatched.

A GIANT'S STEPS

Like many of its sauropod cousins, *Argentinosaurus* really pushed the boundaries of terrestrial size limits. Being so big and so heavy, it could only walk at a top speed of 4.9 miles per hour, and its joints had huge cartilage "cushions" to help protect them from damage. Massive vertebrae and pillar-like legs helped support its bulk.

This enormous fossilised *Argentinosaurus* rib gives an idea of its vast size.

HESPERORNIS

HES-peh-ROR-nis

MEANING: "Western bird"
PERIOD: Late Cretaceous
LOCALITY: North America, Asia
LENGTH: 3.9-4.9 ft
WEIGHT: 44 lbs
DIET: Fish, squid

This close relative of modern birds still had jaws lined with serrated teeth like those of its theropod ancestors, but they sat in long grooves rather than individual sockets. *Hesperornis* is known from several species, and fished the rich northern seas, using its hind limbs to propel it through the water.

An adult *Hesperornis* scans the nearby shore, looking for potential predators and prey.

TOOTHY BEAK

Hesperornis had a birdlike beak, but its jaws were lined with small, serrated teeth that helped snag marine prey.

However, life in the Mesozoic oceans was often perilous, and as well as being a predator, *Hesperornis* was often prey for larger animals itself. One juvenile *Hesperornis* fossil shows bite marks along its lower leg that match the jaws of a young plesiosaur. Luckily for this individual, it appears that it managed to wriggle away from the hungry marine reptile.

ADAPTED FOR WATER

Hesperornis' wings were tiny and useless for flight, but its stubby arms helped make its body more streamlined. It also showed some similarities to modern diving birds like auks (left) and penguins: its legs were positioned at the back of its body, and the shape of its toe bones meant *Hesperornis* probably had lobed feet like grebes, a type of modern-day water bird. Its sprawling legs were ideal for swimming, but returning to land to lay eggs was probably very difficult, and it may have moved around on its belly like a seal.

PROTOCERATOPS

PROH-toe-SEH-ruh-tops

MEANING: "First horned face"
PERIOD: Late Cretaceous
LOCALITY: Mongolia
LENGTH: 6.5 ft
WEIGHT: 330 lbs
DIET: Herbivore

Protoceratops is known from a variety of specimens ranging from unhatched embryos to full-grown adults. Due to the good preservation of this material, this herbivore has been well studied, and scientists have learned a lot about its growth, development, and social behavior as it ambled around Late Cretaceous Mongolia.

FOSSIL FIGHT

One of the most spectacular fossils ever discovered consists of a *Protoceratops* locked in battle with a *Velociraptor*. The two were probably buried by a collapsing sand dune, preserving their struggle for over 80 million years. Unfortunately there is no way to be sure of the reason for the fight, and several ideas are equally plausible. For example, the predatory *Velociraptor* might have been hunting the *Protoceratops,* or this may have been a dispute over space or other resources.

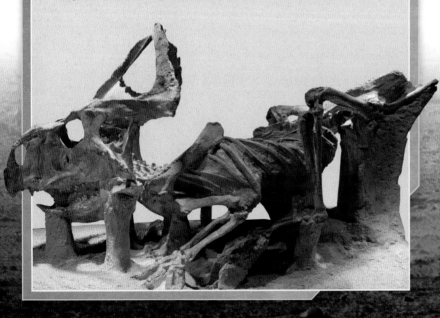

ATTRACTING MATES

Young *Protoceratops* lacked frills, but as they got older the frills grew faster compared to other parts of their bodies. The animal's frill was most probably used to attract a mate, with its cheek horns and deep tail perhaps adding to the impressive effect. Like most dinosaurs, *Protoceratops* was able to mate before it reached full size.

Protoceratops' tail was short but provided some counterbalance.

REPTILE-LIKE INCUBATION

The growth lines in the teeth of *Protoceratops* embryos suggest that this species needed a mimimum of 83 days to incubate their eggs, which they laid in simple nests. This is faster than the average modern reptile (100 days), but slower than a typical bird (40 days). It is most similar to crocodilians (80 days).

101

PTERANODON

TER-an-OH-don

MEANING: 'Toothless wing'
PERIOD: Late Cretaceous
LOCALITY: North America
WINGSPAN: 7m
WEIGHT: 45kg
DIET: Carnivore

Well over a thousand specimens of this pterosaur have been found, making it one of the best-known extinct species. *Pteranodon* flew and hunted over an ancient stretch of sea known as the Western Interior Seaway, which cut North America in half. This sea has since disappeared, but the remains of a vibrant ocean community have been unearthed from the rocks.

Gliding on the air currents, this male *Pteranodon* heads out to sea in search of fish.

SEAFOOD DIET

Fossilised fish bones have been found in the stomachs of several individual *Pteranodon*. They were probably excellent soarers, and could travel long distances in search of food. They may even have been able to take off from the water, using their powerful chest muscles to launch from the surface.

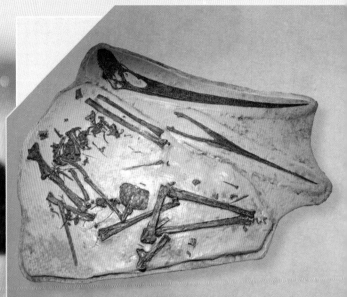

FOSSIL SEXES

Pteranodon fossils show that this species came in two basic sizes: larger individuals with long crests, and smaller ones sporting a stubby, rounded crest. This is probably a difference between males and females, with the large crests perhaps used as a display structure to attract mates.

WEIGHTY ISSUES

Figuring out the weight of flying reptiles is very tricky, and estimates for *Pteranodon* have ranged from 35 lbs to over 198 lbs. Many studies used modern bats and birds as a comparison point to figure out the size of pterosaurs, but the big differences in anatomy mean the estimates are probably inaccurate. It's generally agreed that the higher estimates for *Pteranodon* are too heavy, and future research using other techniques might offer more precise insights.

103

CARNOTAURUS

CAR-no-TOR-us

MEANING: "Meat-eating bull"
PERIOD: Late Cretaceous
LOCALITY: South America
LENGTH: 25 ft
WEIGHT: 2.2 tons
DIET: Carnivore

Carnotaurus' short skull and the distinctive horns above its eyes make it one of the most recognizable theropod dinosaurs. The horns gave it its name, as "taurus" is Latin for "bull." It prowled the Late Cretaceous of South America.

PREHISTORIC WRESTLING

The brow horns above each eye were perhaps used to shove other *Carnotaurus* when competing over mates, food, or territory. Analysis of the skull shows that it probably didn't deliver rapid head blows, as these would have caused too much damage. *Carnotaurus'* slender lower jaw meant it couldn't deliver more powerful bites, but *Carnotaurus* could shut its mouth much faster than other theropods like *Allosaurus.* As a result, it may have preferred hunting smaller prey.

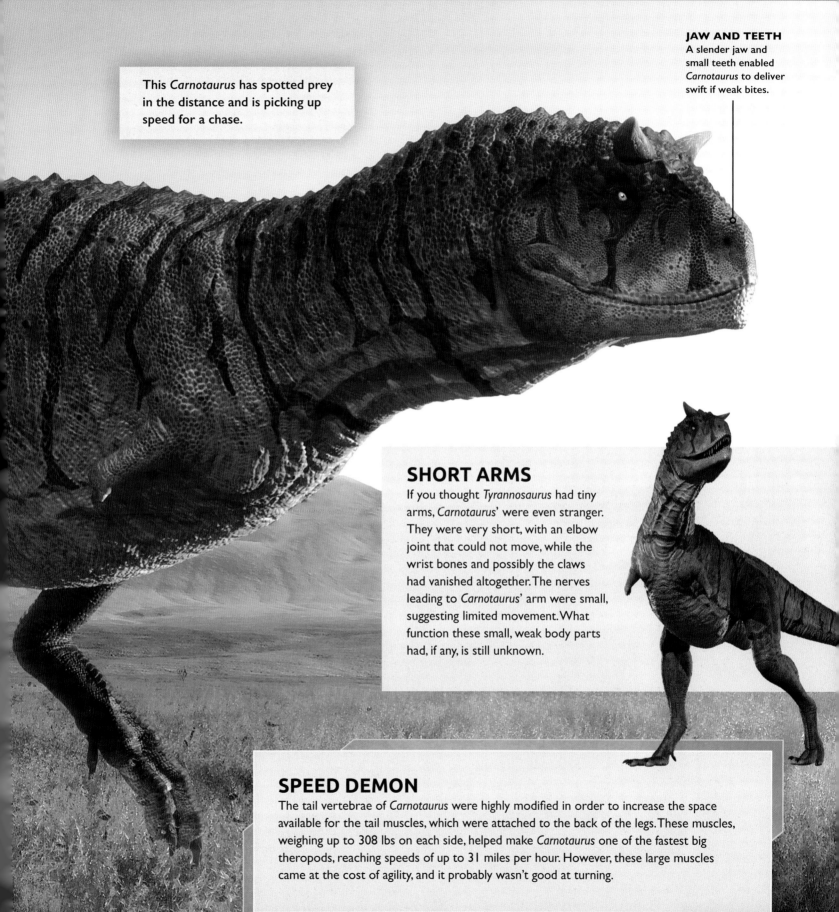

JAW AND TEETH
A slender jaw and small teeth enabled *Carnotaurus* to deliver swift if weak bites.

This *Carnotaurus* has spotted prey in the distance and is picking up speed for a chase.

SHORT ARMS

If you thought *Tyrannosaurus* had tiny arms, *Carnotaurus*' were even stranger. They were very short, with an elbow joint that could not move, while the wrist bones and possibly the claws had vanished altogether. The nerves leading to *Carnotaurus*' arm were small, suggesting limited movement. What function these small, weak body parts had, if any, is still unknown.

SPEED DEMON

The tail vertebrae of *Carnotaurus* were highly modified in order to increase the space available for the tail muscles, which were attached to the back of the legs. These muscles, weighing up to 308 lbs on each side, helped make *Carnotaurus* one of the fastest big theropods, reaching speeds of up to 31 miles per hour. However, these large muscles came at the cost of agility, and it probably wasn't good at turning.

105

PARASAUROLOPHUS
pah-ra-SOR-oh-LO-fus

MEANING: "Near crested lizard"
PERIOD: Late Cretaceous
LOCALITY: North America
LENGTH: 31 ft
WEIGHT: 2.2-4.9 tons
DIET: Herbivore

The flamboyant *Parasaurolophus* is best known for the large tube-like crest ornamenting a skull that was over 6.5 ft long in some species. Its curved beak would have helped it crop vegetation, and some fossil specimens are well enough preserved to show imprints of its scaly skin.

SCAN THIS PAGE

CREST GROWTH

Parasaurolophus was a crested hadrosaur, and most such creatures only developed their crests once their skulls had reached around half their maximum size. In *Parasaurolophus*, however, this occurred at a much younger age, which may be why its crest reached huge sizes in adulthood.

CREST
Parasaurolophus had the largest crest of any hadrosaur.

MOUTH
A tough beak, made out of keratin, snipped off vegetation.

CHEEK POUCHES
Hadrosaurs may have had some form of "cheeks" to help keep the plant matter in their mouths while they chewed.

SCAN THIS PAGE

WATCH IT NOW
See Parasaurolophus in action by viewing this page in the app.

Devonian 419-359 MYA	Carboniferous 359-299 MYA	Permian 299-252 MYA	Triassic 252-201 MYA	Jurassic 201-145 MYA	Cretaceous 145-66 MYA	Paleogene 66-23 MYA	Neogene 23-3 MYA
Paleozoic 541-252 MYA			Mesozoic 252-66 MYA			Cenozoic 66-0 MYA	

CREST FUNCTION

Recent research suggest that *Parasaurolophus*' tubed crest played a role in communication. The long, folded nasal passage inside it may have let *Parasaurolophus* create low sounds—although given its extremely large size, it may have been used for display as well.

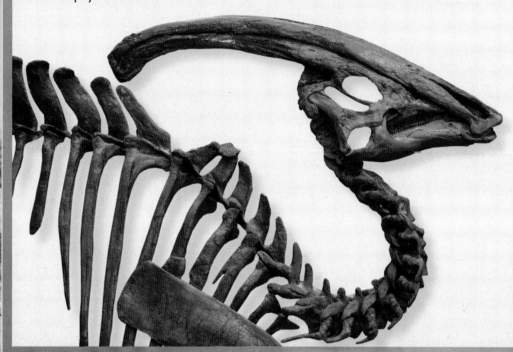

WATER DWELLER?

Some scientists used to think that this huge crest was a snorkel, or was studded with nerve endings that could smell out edible plants! However we're now certain that *Parasaurolophus* was a land animal.

HOW MANY SPECIES OF *PARASAUROLOPHUS* WERE THERE?

Three species are currently known, whose crests and internal passageways vary in shape and size. A fourth animal, *Charonosaurus* from Asia, might also be a type of *Parasaurolophus*.

HOW QUICKLY DID *PARASAUROLOPHUS* GROW?

Juveniles were already up to 32 percent of their adult size within their first year, and weighed several hundred pounds.

DID OTHER HADROSAURS HAVE CRESTS?

These herbivores evolved all sorts of crest designs, and they were used in similar ways to help communicate, either visually or by sound. Some were made of bone, while others had fleshy structures like a cockerel's comb.

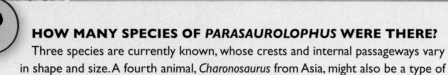

109

CITIPATI

CHIT-i-puh-tih

MEANING: "Funeral pyre lord"
PERIOD: Late Cretaceous
LOCALITY: Mongolia
LENGTH: 9.8 ft
WEIGHT: 154 lbs
DIET: Herbivore

Let's set the scene: the days are warm in Late Cretaceous Mongolia, and a relatively small theropod can be found sitting on its nest, covering its eggs with its outstretched arms. This attentive parent was a *Citipati*—a type of oviraptorosaur—which suddenly died while tending to its nest, engulfed by a sandstorm or buried under a collapsing sand dune. This fossilized scene provides an intimate look at the evolution of nesting behaviors we see in birds today.

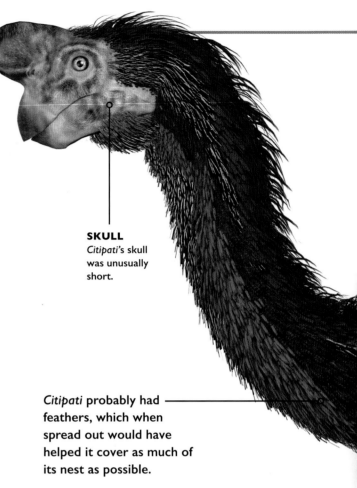

SKULL
Citipati's skull was unusually short.

Citipati probably had feathers, which when spread out would have helped it cover as much of its nest as possible.

BIG SITTERS

Citipati laid its eggs in a circle, and sat in the middle so as not to crush them. Whether this was to incubate them, shelter them, or protect them against predators is still uncertain. As these dinosaurs grew larger, so did the space in the center of the nest, allowing even the biggest oviraptorosaurs, which weighed over a ton, to brood their nests.

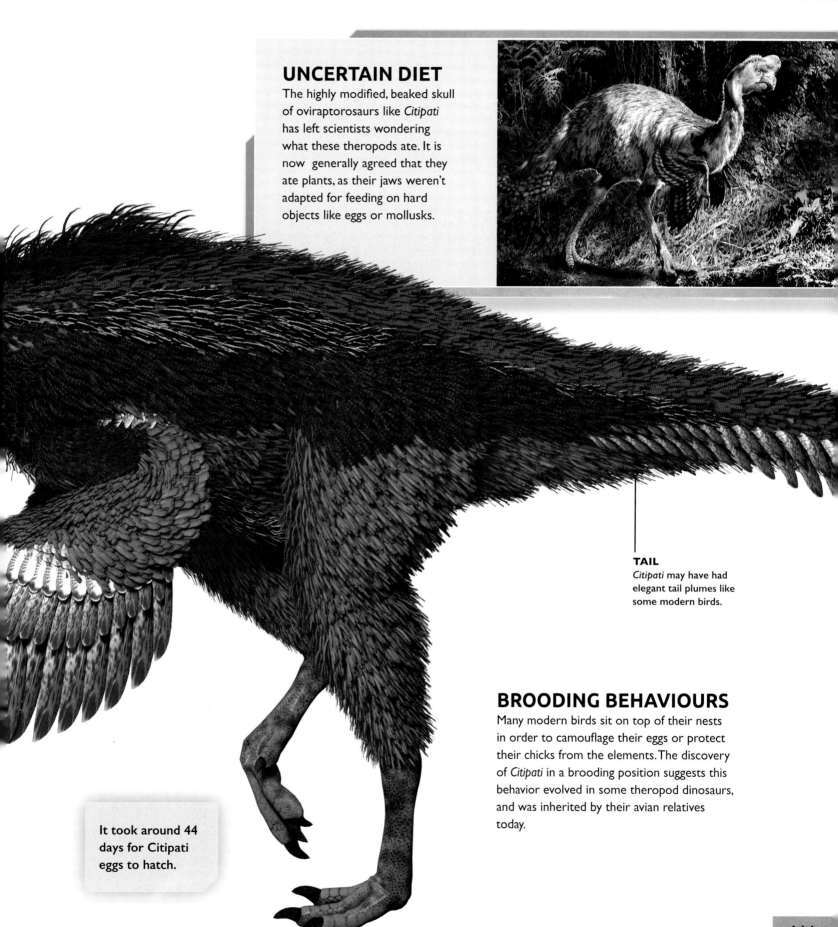

| Devonian 419-359 MYA | Carboniferous 359-299 MYA | Permian 299-252 MYA | Triassic 252-201 MYA | Jurassic 201-145 MYA | Cretaceous 145-66 MYA | Paleogene 66-23 MYA | Neogene 23-3 MYA |

| Paleozoic 541-252 MYA | | | Mesozoic 252-66 MYA | | | Cenozoic 66-0 MYA | |

UNCERTAIN DIET

The highly modified, beaked skull of oviraptorosaurs like *Citipati* has left scientists wondering what these theropods ate. It is now generally agreed that they ate plants, as their jaws weren't adapted for feeding on hard objects like eggs or mollusks.

TAIL
Citipati may have had elegant tail plumes like some modern birds.

BROODING BEHAVIOURS

Many modern birds sit on top of their nests in order to camouflage their eggs or protect their chicks from the elements. The discovery of *Citipati* in a brooding position suggests this behavior evolved in some theropod dinosaurs, and was inherited by their avian relatives today.

It took around 44 days for Citipati eggs to hatch.

EDMONTOSAURUS

Ed-MON-to-SOR-us

MEANING: "Lizard from Edmonton"
PERIOD: Late Cretaceous
LOCALITY: North America
LENGTH: 29-42 ft
WEIGHT: 4.4-7.6 tons
DIET: Herbivore

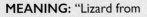

The much-studied herbivore *Edmontosaurus* was the largest ornithopod to inhabit Late Cretaceous North America, where it roamed subtropical coastal areas of modern-day Canada and the United States. Although predominantly a four-legged animal, it's possible that this giant reared up on two legs depending on the situation. It fed on a variety of tough plants like conifer needles, and even occasionally tree bark.

BEAK ISSUES

Despite *Edmontosaurus*' "duck-billed" snout bones—which made many early paleontologists think it lived in swamps feeding on water plants—some very well-preserved specimens show it would actually have had a large, down-turned beak. This might have been useful for cropping tough terrestrial vegetation.

Edmontosaurus had hundreds of small teeth, arranged in stacks lining the back of the jaws, which helped grind down tough plants.

SOCIAL GATHERINGS

Many individual *Edmontosaurus* have been found in several deposits of fossils, suggesting that it lived in herds. In the northern parts of its range, some researchers have suggested Alaskan *Edmontosaurus* migrated several thousand miles south to escape six months of darkness and bitter winter chill. However, other studies suggest that it may have overwintered in the cold north, slowing down its growth rates as food became scarce.

SOFT TISSUE

As well as finding numerous skeletons, paleontologists have unearthed skin impressions for *Edmontosaurus*, revealing that at least one species had a small, soft crest, similar to that of a cockerel. Paleontologists aren't sure whether this was found in all *Edmontosaurus* species, or just a single one. It may have been used to attract mates.

113

MAJUNGASAURUS

Mah-JOON-guh-SOR-us

MEANING: "Mahajanga lizard"
PERIOD: Late Cretaceous
LOCALITY: Africa
LENGTH: 18–22 ft
WEIGHT: 1.6 tons
DIET: Carnivore

By the end of the Cretaceous period, the island of Madagascar had long been fully separated from the African mainland. As it is today, Madagascar was home to a diverse range of creatures, including giant frogs, terrestrial relatives of modern crocodilians, and dinosaurs. *Majungasaurus* was the largest predator in the region, with some fragmentary remains suggesting it grew larger than the 18 ft calculated for most known individuals.

TEXTURED SKULL

The rough patches of bone that covered the surface of *Majungasaurus*' knobbly skull indicate this predator had tough, keratin-rich skin. A hollow horn jutted out from the top of its skull, which, combined with its huge neck muscles, might have been used during combat.

BIRDLIKE BREATHING

Like its cousins *Carnotaurus* and *Ceratosaurus*, *Majungasaurus* was a ceratosaur, a kind of primitive theropod that was more distantly related to birds than were theropods like *Tyrannosaurus* or *Velociraptor*. However, holes in the vertebrae and parts of the ribs similar to theropods and sauropods show this dinosaur would have had a system of air sacs. These are seen in modern birds today, but developed long before birds first evolved, and provided a very efficient way of breathing.

An apex predator, *Majungasaurus* had more teeth than almost any other abelisaurid.

TAIL
Like all abelisaurids, its large tail provided a counterweight for its stocky frame, allowing it to walk on two legs.

HANDS
Its small hands were immobile, unlike *T. rex*'s.

ISLAND CANNIBAL

Several *Majungasaurus* bones have been found bearing tooth marks that match *Majungasaurus*' own teeth, showing that while sauropod meat may have been on the menu, these carnivores were certainly hungry enough to feed on one another. Whether they hunted their fellows or scavenged their carcasses is less certain.

THERIZINOSAURUS
Ther-ih-ZEEN-oh-SOR-us

MEANING: "Scythe lizard"
PERIOD: Late Cretaceous
LOCALITY: Mongolia
LENGTH: 32.8 ft
WEIGHT: 4,409 lbs
DIET: Herbivore

Sporting the longest claws of any known animal, the pot-bellied *Therizinosaurus* was a Late Cretaceous giant. Along with the more famous *Velociraptor*, it belonged to a wider group known as the maniraptorans. Given its huge size, it is easily the largest maniraptoran currently known to science.

WIDE HIPS

During theropod evolution, many different groups changed their diets, moving from a carnivorous lifestyle to plant-based in the case of the therizinosaurs. We only have fragmentary remains of *Therizinosaurus*, but based on the hipbones of other therizinosaurs, it is likely the animal had a very wide pelvic region in order to house a huge gut, which is useful when digesting plant material.

MISSING ELEMENTS

As it is known only from a few bones, including the giant hand claws, scientists have to study other therizinosaurs to get a better picture of what *Therizinosaurus* looked like. It probably had a small, beaked head and a long neck that it used to forage for vegetation. As many of its theropod cousins had feathers, *Therizinosaurus* probably did too.

CLAW FUNCTIONS

Therizinosaurs increased the size of their claws as they evolved, until *Therizinosaurus* ended up with claws 3 feet long. Just what these were used for is still unknown. Some analyses suggest that they were not designed for digging, but were rather effective when pulling objects toward the body. They could well have been used to reach out and snag plants.

PACHYCEPHALOSAURUS

PAK-ee-SEF-a-lo-SOR-us

MEANING: "Thick-headed lizard"
PERIOD: Late Cretaceous
LOCALITY: North America
LENGTH: 16 ft
WEIGHT: 992 lbs
DIET: Omnivore

SCAN
THIS PAGE

The dome-headed *Pachycephalosaurus*, which trotted around North America in the Late Cretaceous, was distantly related to *Triceratops*. It's known from very few remains, sparking debate about how this animal grew and fed, but its short arms meant it was bipedal.

Pachycephalosaurus may have used its dome against predators as well as members of its own species.

FIGHTING SPIRIT

Pachycephalosaurus is notable for its 9.8-in-thick skull. These animals probably used to clash their heads together, as injuries and infections have been found on the domes of several individuals. The dome was made up of a unique type of bone that healed quickly, a useful adaptation if the animals often clashed heads. But few other bones have been found, meaning that we don't know if *Pachycephalosaurus* also fought in other ways.

SMALL HANDS
Pachycephalosaurus had five-fingered hands.

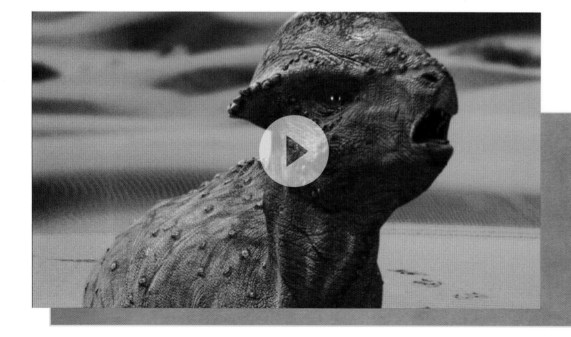

SCAN THIS PAGE

WATCH IT NOW
See Pachycephalosaurus in action by viewing this page in the app.

Devonian 419-359 MYA	Carboniferous 359-299 MYA	Permian 299-252 MYA	Triassic 252-201 MYA	Jurassic 201-145 MYA	Cretaceous 145-66 MYA	Paleogene 66-23 MYA	Neogene 23-3 MYA

Paleozoic 541-252 MYA	Mesozoic 252-66 MYA	Cenozoic 66-0 MYA

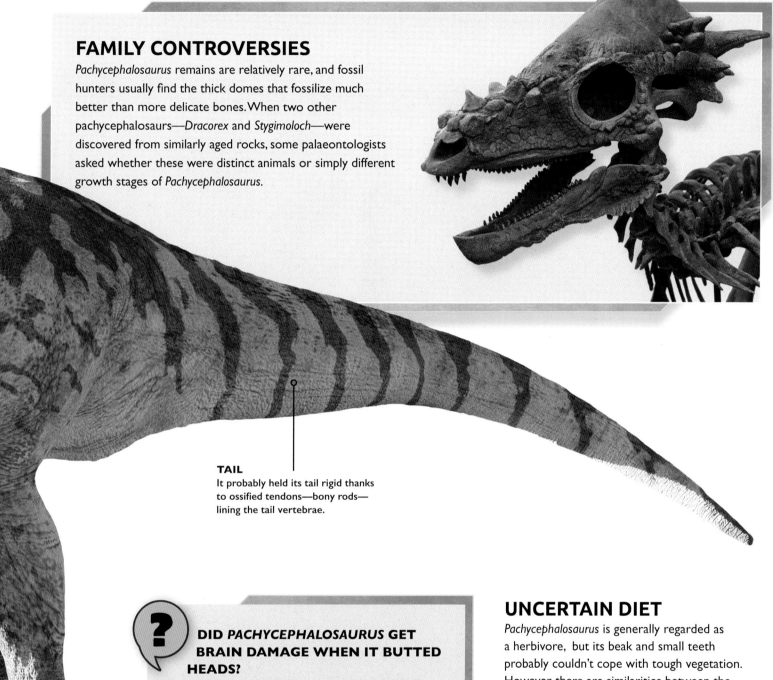

FAMILY CONTROVERSIES

Pachycephalosaurus remains are relatively rare, and fossil hunters usually find the thick domes that fossilize much better than more delicate bones. When two other pachycephalosaurs—*Dracorex* and *Stygimoloch*—were discovered from similarly aged rocks, some palaeontologists asked whether these were distinct animals or simply different growth stages of *Pachycephalosaurus*.

TAIL
It probably held its tail rigid thanks to ossified tendons—bony rods—lining the tail vertebrae.

? **DID *PACHYCEPHALOSAURUS* GET BRAIN DAMAGE WHEN IT BUTTED HEADS?**
As we don't have any brains to check for damage, it's hard to say. It also depends on how often these dinosaurs fought one another, and whether injuries to their brains affected them in the same way they affect us. So we will probably never know.

HOW FAST DID IT RUN?
Some scientists think it could reach 14.9 miles per hour as it butted its skull against a rival's.

UNCERTAIN DIET

Pachycephalosaurus is generally regarded as a herbivore, but its beak and small teeth probably couldn't cope with tough vegetation. However, there are similarities between the front teeth of one fossilized specimen and those of carnivorous theropods. Perhaps it was an omnivore, eating both plants and meat.

DAKOTARAPTOR
Dah-KOE-ta-RAP-tor

MEANING: "Thief of Dakota"
PERIOD: Late Cretaceous
LOCALITY: North America
LENGTH: 16-19 ft
WEIGHT: 824 lbs
DIET: Carnivore

SCAN THIS PAGE

Dakotaraptor towered over most of its relatives among the dromaeosaurids, small- to medium-sized feathered theropods of whom the best known is the sickle-clawed, turkey-sized *Velociraptor*. A large body size brought the advantages of tackling larger prey, and *Dakotaraptor* probably feasted on young and adolescent herbivores.

SKULL
No skulls of this predator have yet been found, so paleontologists have to estimate its shape based on the skulls of related species.

TEETH
Small, serrated teeth probably lined its jaws.

AMERICAN PREDATOR

Until the discovery of *Dakotaraptor*, the predators stalking North America 66 million years ago were thought to have come in two general sizes: the immense, 6.6-8.8 ton *Tyrannosaurus*, or the smaller maniraptorans weighing several pounds. The addition of *Dakotaraptor* helped change paleontologists' views of the ancient North American ecosystem, and showed that there were mid-range predators between the two extremes.

SCAN THIS PAGE

WATCH IT NOW
See Dakotaraptor *in motion by viewing this page in the app.*

ECOLOGICAL ROLE

A fully grown *Tyrannosaurus* was 20 times *Dakotaraptor*'s weight, but it might have provided some competition for subadult tyrannosaurs. Yet, even young tyrannosaurs were twice as heavy as *Dakotaraptor*, and were probably already capable of bringing down mid-sized herbivores. *Dakotaraptor* might have preferred attacking young dinosaurs, or used its superior speed to track fast prey.

FEATHERS
As well as display or stability, *Dakotaraptor*'s feathers might have helped keep it warm.

Built for running, *Dakotaraptor* would have been able to pursue its prey at high speeds.

CLAWS
The large "sickle claw" was used to grip prey.

FEATHERED PLUNDERER

Like many of its maniraptoran relatives, *Dakotaraptor* was covered in feathers. Its arm bones were lined with small "quill knobs," which served as attachment points for long feathers. As it was too big to fly, these might have been used when hunting, in order to keep it stable as it pinned its prey to the ground, or as a display.

MOSASAURS

MO-sah-sors

Mosasaurs were a group of marine reptiles who appeared during the Late Cretaceous, 95 million years ago. They were related to modern snakes and lizards, but adopted a fully aquatic way of life. These air-breathing reptiles were great swimmers, and their fossil record spreads across the globe. Quite where they sit in the reptile family tree is unclear, but perhaps their closest living relatives are lizards like the Komodo dragon.

SIZE RANGE

The smallest mosasurs, like *Dallasaurus*, grew to around 3.2 ft in length, while giants like *Mosasaurus* could reach 55 ft. They had scales, possibly a forked tongue, and may even have generated heat internally, like birds and mammals do today.

This mosasaur roams the depths in search of food, but will have to return to the surface to breathe.

CONVERGENT CAMOUFLAGE

Like the ichthyosaurs, and various marine organisms navigating the oceans today, mosasaur soft tissue was probably countershaded, which means it was dark on top, with a lighter underbelly. Like other marine reptiles, mosasaurs' hands and feet were modified to form paddles. Their tails were also shaped into a fluke, which resembled those of sharks, ichthyosaurs, and some marine crocodylomorphs. These convergent adaptations helped them live their entire lives at sea.

JAWS OF THE DEEP

Mosasaurs possessed flexible jaws and a double row of teeth on their palate, similar to some modern snakes and lizards. This allowed them to swallow prey whole, and the stomach contents of several mosasaurs show a varied diet, including fish, seabirds, sharks, turtles, and other marine reptiles. Some preferred a shellfish diet. The round crushing teeth of *Globidens*, for instance, were perfect for cracking the shells of ammonites.

ANKYLOSAURUS

AN-kee-lo-SOR-us

MEANING: "Fused lizard"
PERIOD: Late Cretaceous
LOCALITY: North America
LENGTH: 32 ft
WEIGHT: 8.8 tons
DIET: Herbivore

SCAN THIS PAGE

Once this tanklike herbivore grew to adult size, its sheer bulk, armored skin and impressive tail club made it nearly predator-proof. It may even have had small protective bony plates in its eyelids! Its extremely wide ribcage housed a massive gut to help break down vegetable matter, which it cropped from low-growing plants with its beak.

TINY TEETH AND STRONG TONGUES

Ankylosaurus' head was 29 inches wide, but its teeth were very small. To compensate, it likely had a strong, movable tongue— a rarity amongst dinosaurs— which would have helped grind down vegetation in its mouth to fuel its bulk.

ARMORED PLATES
The knobs on Ankylosaurs' backs are called scutes.

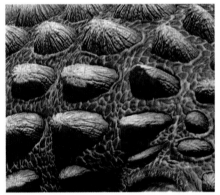

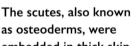
The scutes, also known as osteoderms, were embedded in thick skin.

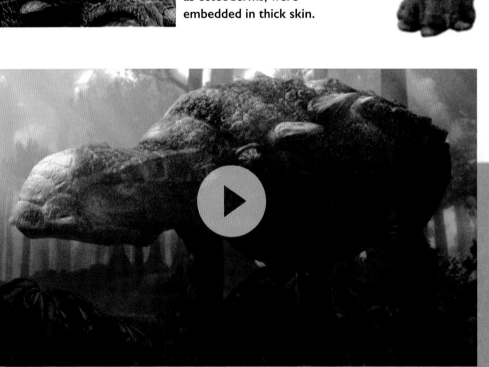

WATCH IT NOW
See Ankylosaurus *in action* by viewing this page in the app.

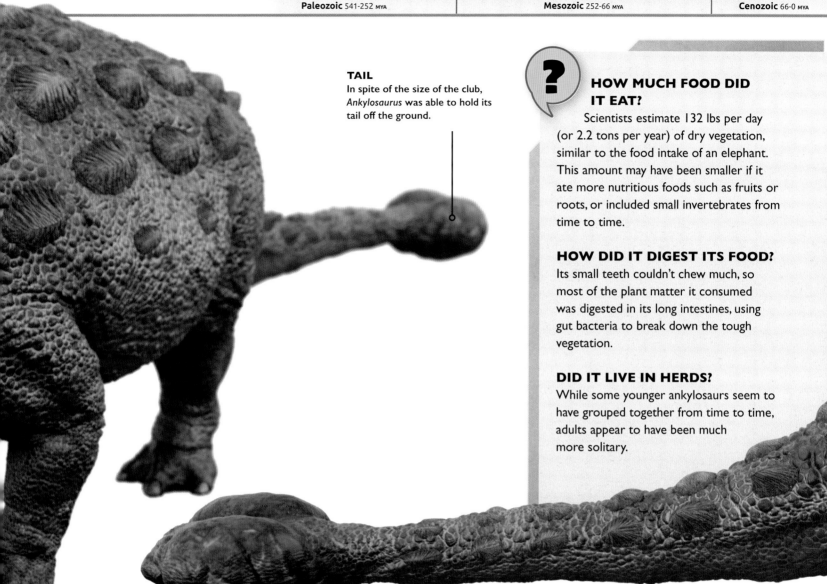

TAIL
In spite of the size of the club, *Ankylosaurus* was able to hold its tail off the ground.

?

HOW MUCH FOOD DID IT EAT?
Scientists estimate 132 lbs per day (or 2.2 tons per year) of dry vegetation, similar to the food intake of an elephant. This amount may have been smaller if it ate more nutritious foods such as fruits or roots, or included small invertebrates from time to time.

HOW DID IT DIGEST ITS FOOD?
Its small teeth couldn't chew much, so most of the plant matter it consumed was digested in its long intestines, using gut bacteria to break down the tough vegetation.

DID IT LIVE IN HERDS?
While some younger ankylosaurs seem to have grouped together from time to time, adults appear to have been much more solitary.

DEFENSIVE CLUBS
The end of *Ankylosaurus'* tail, to which the heavy club was attached, was supported by interlocking vertebrae and ossified tendons (bony rods). The largest clubs could break bone, but scientists don't know whether they used their tails in this way in defence against predators, or to settle disputes among themselves.

COMPLEX AIRWAYS
Within the skull of *Ankylosaurus*, and many other ankylosaurs, was a complex network of looping tubes that made up the nasal passage. This adaptation was probably not used to enhance its sense of smell, but instead helped keep it cool. Big bodies take longer to cool down than smaller ones, and overheating can kill large creatures. These twisting tubes helped speed up the rate at which heat was lost and, as a result, the creature's brain could be kept at a steady temperature.

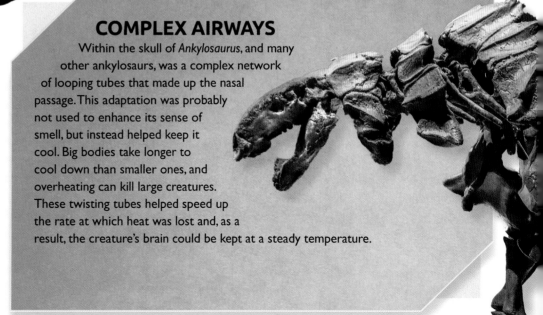

131

QUETZALCOATLUS

KET-sul-kow-AT-luhs

MEANING: "Feathered serpent"
(after the Aztec God Quetzalcoatl)
PERIOD: Late Cretaceous
LOCALITY: North America
WINGSPAN: 36 ft
WEIGHT: 440-573 lbs
DIET: Carnivore

SCAN THIS PAGE

As tall as *Tyrannosaurus* or a modern giraffe, and with a wingspan to rival a small plane, *Quetzalcoatlus* was one of the largest animals to ever take to the skies. It was equally comfortable stalking the ground of Late Cretaceous North America, its huge wings folded against its body. We know of it from the fragmentary remains of two species.

TOO HEAVY FOR TAKE OFF?

Could this giant pterosaur really fly? The current evidence points to an animal that was adept at both walking and flying: its arms are powerful but not modified enough for a fully terrestrial life, the muscle attachment sites on its arm bones are large to help generate power for flight, and the bones are strong enough to cope with the stresses of flying. Whether they spent more time on the ground than in the air is uncertain, and perhaps flight was only used to cover large distances or get away from danger.

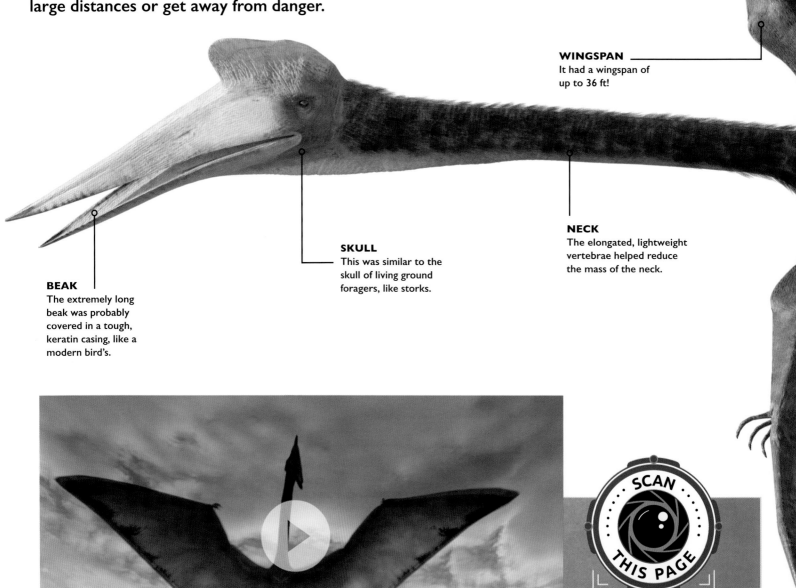

WINGSPAN
It had a wingspan of up to 36 ft!

SKULL
This was similar to the skull of living ground foragers, like storks.

NECK
The elongated, lightweight vertebrae helped reduce the mass of the neck.

BEAK
The extremely long beak was probably covered in a tough, keratin casing, like a modern bird's.

SCAN THIS PAGE

WATCH IT NOW
See Quetzalcoatlus in motion by viewing this page in the app.

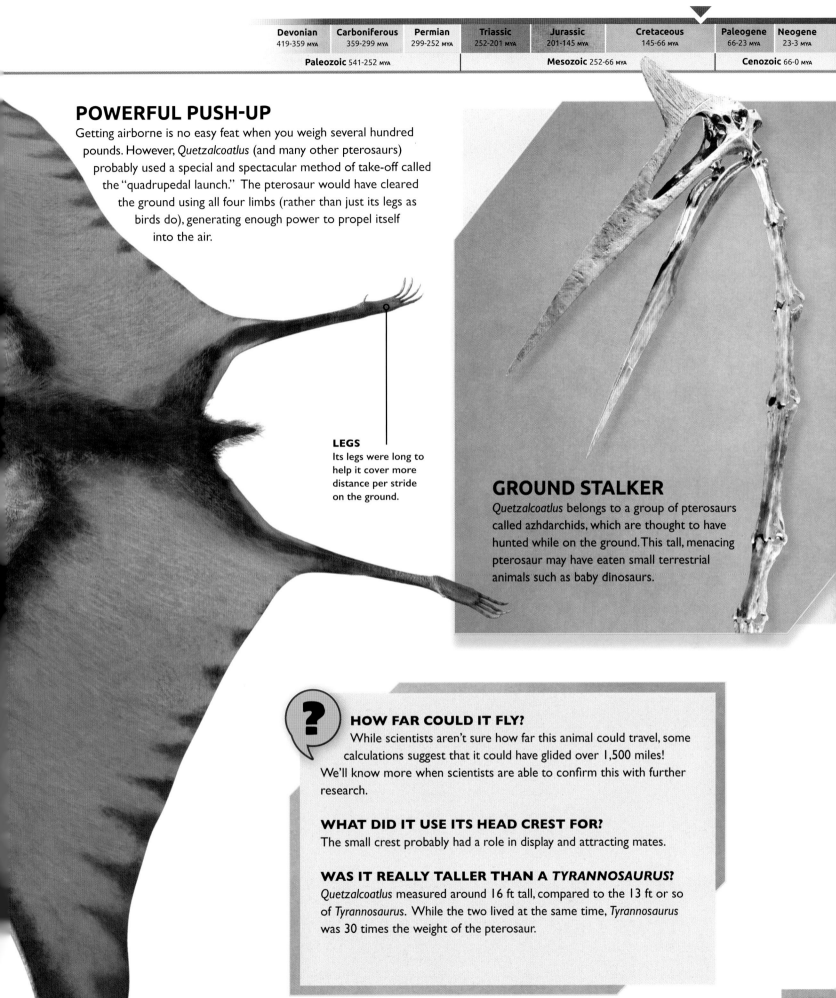

POWERFUL PUSH-UP

Getting airborne is no easy feat when you weigh several hundred pounds. However, *Quetzalcoatlus* (and many other pterosaurs) probably used a special and spectacular method of take-off called the "quadrupedal launch." The pterosaur would have cleared the ground using all four limbs (rather than just its legs as birds do), generating enough power to propel itself into the air.

LEGS
Its legs were long to help it cover more distance per stride on the ground.

GROUND STALKER

Quetzalcoatlus belongs to a group of pterosaurs called azhdarchids, which are thought to have hunted while on the ground. This tall, menacing pterosaur may have eaten small terrestrial animals such as baby dinosaurs.

? HOW FAR COULD IT FLY?
While scientists aren't sure how far this animal could travel, some calculations suggest that it could have glided over 1,500 miles! We'll know more when scientists are able to confirm this with further research.

WHAT DID IT USE ITS HEAD CREST FOR?
The small crest probably had a role in display and attracting mates.

WAS IT REALLY TALLER THAN A *TYRANNOSAURUS*?
Quetzalcoatlus measured around 16 ft tall, compared to the 13 ft or so of *Tyrannosaurus*. While the two lived at the same time, *Tyrannosaurus* was 30 times the weight of the pterosaur.

135

TRICERATOPS

Try-SEH-ra-tops

MEANING: "Three horned face"
PERIOD: Late Cretaceous
LOCALITY: North America
LENGTH: 26-29 ft
WEIGHT: 6.6 tons
DIET: Herbivore

Triceratops, one of the best-known of all dinosaurs, crashed through the forests of Cretaceous North America. Sporting one of the largest skulls of any land animal, this herbivore is known from several hundred specimens, some of which even preserve imprints of its skin.

THREE-HORNED THREAT

Although *Triceratops* is often shown fighting off *Tyrannosaurus* with its horns, scientists now generally agree that the horns and frill probably mainly evolved to attract mates, rather than for defense. However, battle scars have been found on the skulls of *Triceratops*, indicating that these herbivores could settle disputes by locking horns.

GROWING UP

Triceratops fossils range from massive, fully grown adults to small juveniles. As a result, scientists have been able to map the way its skull developed as it grew older. The brow horns changed shape, the nose horn fused to the snout, and the frill lost its spiky edge, becoming smoother.

HORNS
Its brow horns grew up to 3.5 ft long.

SKULL
Triceratops' skull could reach over 6.5 ft long.

FRILL
The neck frill was made by modified skull bones that fused together.

TEETH
Triceratops' jaws contained some of the most complex teeth ever to have evolved, helping it chew up plants.

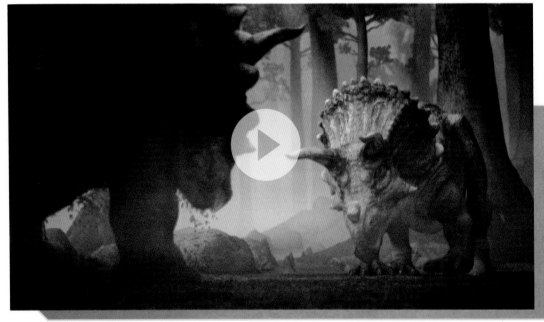

SCAN THIS PAGE

WATCH IT NOW
View this page in the app to see Triceratops in motion.

Devonian	Carboniferous	Permian	Triassic	Jurassic	Cretaceous	Paleogene	Neogene
419-359 MYA	359-299 MYA	299-252 MYA	252-201 MYA	201-145 MYA	145-66 MYA	66-23 MYA	23-3 MYA

Paleozoic 541-252 MYA	Mesozoic 252-66 MYA	Cenozoic 66-0 MYA

Imprints of scaly skin have been found next to skeletons. Some of the scales had small, conical "spikes" projecting from the middle.

? HOW DID *TRICERATOPS* EAT?

Triceratops had hundreds of teeth arranged in rows known as "dental batteries." After nipping off low-lying vegetation with its beak, the leaves, flowers, and branches would be ground down by its powerful jaws.

DID *TRICERATOPS* EVER REALLY FIGHT *TYRANNOSAURUS*?

Both dinosaurs lived during the same time, and one fossil in particular shows a broken brow horn caused by a *T. rex* bite. It healed, indicating the herbivore survived the fight.

HOW MANY SPECIES OF *TRICERATOPS* WERE THERE?

Two species are currently recognized: *Triceratops horridus* and *Triceratops prorsus*. They lived during separate parts of the late Cretaceous and never shared an ecosystem.

LONE RANGER?

While several ceratopsians are known from fossil beds containing many individuals, *Triceratops* are often found as single specimens. However, three juveniles have been found together in the same quarry. It may be that younger individuals formed small social groups, becoming less social as they grew older.

Two *Triceratops* face off against one another in a dangerous display of strength.

TYRANNOSAURUS

TY-ran-OH-sor-us

MEANING: "Tyrant lizard"
PERIOD: Late Cretaceous
LOCALITY: North America
LENGTH: 41 ft
WEIGHT: 6.6-9.9 tons
DIET: Carnivore

Arguably the most famous of all the dinosaurs, *Tyrannosaurus* was a massive, bone-crushing predator. It evolved a few million years before the mass extinction at the end of the Cretaceous and was the top predator of its time, with the only competition for prey and other resources coming from other large individuals of its species.

KILLER BITE

While a select few other theropods rivaled *Tyrannosaurus* in size, none were capable of generating similar bite forces. With its jaw-closing muscles generating 4.4 tons of force, it was easily capable of crushing bone. *Tyrannosaurus*' skull was adapted to deal with the stress of biting, with some of the snout bones fused together for strength, while the thick, banana-shaped teeth were less prone to breakage compared to the thinner dentition of other theropods.

JAW
Tyrannosaurus had the strongest bite force of any terrestrial animal, modern or extinct.

SMALL ARMS
Its arms were small but strong, and may have been used to hold struggling prey.

SCAN THIS PAGE

WATCH IT NOW
See Tyrannosaurus *in action by viewing this page in the app.*

SOCIAL PREDATORS?

A set of footprints, most likely belonging to *Tyrannosaurus*, were found showing three individuals moving together in a group. This is evidence that big tyrannosaurs did spend at least some of the time together in groups, but they probably didn't hunt in packs like modern wolves and lions.

FIGHT CLUB

Tyrannosaurus and its close relatives are often found with gouges on their skull bones. These are bite marks, and they have been recorded on juveniles as well as full-grown adults. Just what the animals were arguing about is uncertain, but food, territory, and mating rights are all good candidates. Some injuries show signs of healing, while others were made at or after the time of death, indicating cannibalism.

TAIL
The counterbalancing tail helped keep *Tyrannosaurus* stable when moving.

FOOT
The foot probably helped pin food to the ground while the animal tore chunks out of its prey with its teeth.

Most other animals would have fled at the sight of a *Tyrannosaurus*.

?

DID *TYRANNOSAURUS* ROAR?
In spite of what you see in films, *Tyrannosaurus* and other dinosaurs did not roar like lions. Many probably communicated by making noises with their mouths closed, as well as using visual displays.

WAS IT A PREDATOR OR A SCAVENGER?
It was mainly a hunter, but like most modern carnivores it wouldn't have passed up an easy meal if camea across a carcass.

HOW LONG DID *TYRANNOSAURUS* LIVE?
The oldest known *Tyrannosaurus* was about 30 years old when it died. Hunting big prey and fighting other predators is a dangerous lifestyle, and most died young.

143

CENOZOIC ERA

66–0 million years ago

Although there was a huge extinction event at the end of the Cretaceous, many of the smaller animal forms survived into the Cenozoic Era. Mammals in particular flourished after the disappearance of the non-avian dinosaurs, evolving into new terrestrial, aquatic, and flying types.

Birds, too, were successful, and represent the only surviving dinosaur descendants. They developed into the ten thousand different species alive today. That's more than twice the number of species of modern mammals, making birds the most numerous vertebrate group after the bony fishes. Grass, which started out in the Mesozoic but became extremely successful during the later parts of the Cenozoic, also had a big impact on terrestrial animals' feeding habits.

Although the climate was initially warm, the later parts of the Cenozoic experienced long-term cooling, leading up to Ice Ages that saw much of the Northern Hemisphere gripped in freezing conditions. The evolution of modern humans has also had a profound impact on the world. Not only have we hunted animals to extinction, the rise in human industry has caused temperatures to rapidly climb. This global warming means the world today is knocking on the door of a new mass extinction, and if humans don't change their ways, vast numbers of living things will disappear forever.

TITANOBOA
Ty-TAN-oh-BO-ah

MEANING: "Titanic boa"
PERIOD: Paleocene
LOCALITY: Colombia
LENGTH: 43 ft
WEIGHT: 1.2 tons
DIET: Carnivore

A huge relative of modern day boa constrictors, *Titanoboa* slithered through swampy, humid jungles less than 10 million years after the extinction of the dinosaurs. Its great size meant that it was probably the top predator in its ecosystem.

This *Titanoboa* is using its giant coils to crush its reptilian prey.

CONSTRICTOR FEEDING

Its close relationship to modern boas means scientists are pretty certain how *Titanoboa* fed. It would have used its immensely powerful trunk muscles to crush and suffocate as it coiled around its prey. It would then have swallowed its meal head first, using a jaw joint that allowed it to open its mouth wide.

MAKING A GIANT

As they rely on their environment for heat, the largest modern reptiles are found near the equator, where it's warmest. One of the reasons *Titanoboa* got so big might have been the very warm Paleocene climate, allowing this snake to be more active and reach over a ton in weight. Alternatively, it may be the lack of mammalian competitors that allowed *Titanoboa* to grow so large.

Devonian 419-359 MYA	Carboniferous 359-299 MYA	Permian 299-252 MYA	Triassic 252-201 MYA	Jurassic 201-145 MYA	Cretaceous 145-66 MYA	Paleogene 66-23 MYA	Neogene 23-3 MYA
Paleozoic 541-252 MYA			Mesozoic 252-66 MYA			Cenozoic 66-0 MYA	

BASILOSAURUS

BA-sil-oh-SOR-us

MEANING: "King lizard"
PERIOD: Paleocene
LOCALITY: North Africa,
North America, Middle East
LENGTH: 59 ft
WEIGHT: 7.1 tons
DIET: Carnivore

Initially described as a reptile,
Basilosaurus was in fact a huge,
ocean-going whale. It still had
tiny hind limbs that it inherited
from its terrestrial ancestors, but
it used its powerful fluked tail
to push itself through the water.
Like all whales, it breathed air
and had to come to the surface
to refill its lungs.

VORACIOUS APPETITE

Stomach contents from an Egyptian
Basilosaurus show it ate other whales and
large fish. Its powerful jaw muscles could
close with over 2 tons of force, making
it one of the strongest biting mammals
known. As a result, it could probably
crush bone, and might have aimed for the
head of its potential prey.

DIVING INTO THE DEEP

Although *Basilosaurus* swam the ancient oceans of the northern hemisphere,
it was probably not a good diver. It has been estimated that *Basilosaurus* could
hold its breath for a little over 17 minutes, which is roughly the same as
some modern dolphins, but nowhere near the 2 hours seen in deep-diving
sperm whales. As a result, it probably hunted near the surface.

This shoal of *Basilosaurus*
is on the hunt in the wide
blue Cenozoic ocean.

Devonian	Carboniferous	Permian	Triassic	Jurassic	Cretaceous	Paleogene	Neogene
419-359 MYA	359-299 MYA	299-252 MYA	252-201 MYA	201-145 MYA	145-66 MYA	66-23 MYA	23-3 MYA
Paleozoic 541-252 MYA			Mesozoic 252-66 MYA			Cenozoic 66-0 MYA	

PHORUSRHACOS

FOR-as-RAH-koss

MEANING: "Wrinkle bearer"
PERIOD: Neogene
LOCALITY: Argentina
LENGTH: 8.2 ft
WEIGHT: 287 lbs
DIET: Carnivore

Informally known as the "terror birds," the phorusrhacids were large, flightless predators that stalked the Americas, Antarctica, and Africa during the Cenozoic. One of the largest was *Phorusrhacos*, a South American killer with a skull measuring over 23 inches long, terminating in a vicious, meat-stripping hooked bill.

LIMITED FINDS

Palaeontologists haven't found much of the skeleton of this predator, and reconstructions of the skull are based on a field sketch of a complete specimen that unfortunately crumbled before it could be safely brought back to a museum. As a result, ideas about its way of life are often based on closely related species.

SKULL SCIENCE

Computer simulations of the skull of *Andalgalornis*, a close relative of *Phorusrhacos* that possessed a similar-shaped head, show that these predators either attacked small prey, or used repeated strikes against larger prey, retreating often to get out of harm's way.

STRONG LEGS
The strong legs of phorusrhacids were useful for running, and possibly also for kicking, and clawing open carcasses.

Devonian 419-359 MYA	Carboniferous 359-299 MYA	Permian 299-252 MYA	Triassic 252-201 MYA	Jurassic 201-145 MYA	Cretaceous 145-66 MYA	Paleogene 66-23 MYA	Neogene 23-3 MYA
Paleozoic 541-252 MYA			Mesozoic 252-66 MYA			Cenozoic 66-0 MYA	

OTODUS

Oh-TOE-dus

MEANING: "Ear-shaped tooth"
PERIOD: Paleocene to Neogene
LOCALITY: Worldwide
LENGTH: 32-59 ft
WEIGHT: 13-65 tons
DIET: Carnivore

More commonly known by its species name, *Megalodon*, this giant shark was one of the largest fish to ever exist, probably exceeding the modern whale shark in size. Like many sharks, its cartilaginous skeleton often didn't fossilize. However its teeth were harder and are relatively commonly found.

Great white shark's tooth

Megalodon's tooth

POWER JAWS

Otodus' jaws were over 6.5 ft wide and could generate huge amounts of power. Scientists measured the bite force of living great white sharks to estimate the biting power of the much larger *Otodus*, and revealed mind-blowing statistics: *Otodus* could bite down with 20 tons of force, around ten times that of the largest great white and almost five times that of *Tyrannosaurus*!

COMPETITIVE SEAS

Otodus probably hunted a wide range of species, including whales. However, it might have faced tough competition from another giant predator, *Livyatan*. Related to modern-day sperm whales, *Livyatan* patrolled the seas alone and possessed huge, bone-breaking teeth. Whether the two animals were direct competitors is uncertain, however. They might have swum in different parts of the sea and never met.

This huge *Otodus* bears the scars of fights with prey.

Devonian	Carboniferous	Permian	Triassic	Jurassic	Cretaceous	Paleogene	Neogene
419-359 MYA	359-299 MYA	299-252 MYA	252-201 MYA	201-145 MYA	145-66 MYA	66-23 MYA	23-3 MYA
Paleozoic 541-252 MYA				Mesozoic 252-66 MYA		Cenozoic 66-0 MYA	

COELODONTA

SEE-low-DON-tah

MEANING: "Hollow tooth"
PERIOD: Neogene
LOCALITY: Northern Europe and Asia
LENGTH: 11 ft
WEIGHT: 2.2 tons
DIET: Herbivore

Usually known by its common name, the woolly rhinoceros, *Coelodonta* is one of the iconic Ice Age giants that shared its habitat with early humans. Cave art as well as frozen and mummified remains have helped piece together its appearance, revealing thick fur and two flat horns that protruded from its skull.

Coelodonta needed huge plains to provide it with enough grass to feed its bulk.

ANCIENT DNA

The excellent preservation of some specimens has allowed DNA to be recovered from the fossils. The results indicate that the closest living relative of the woolly rhino is the Sumatran rhinoceros.

GRAZING LIFESTYLE

Coelodonta foraged on low-lying plants, using its broad muzzle to rip up mainly grasses, which it ground to pulp with its large molars. While this animal is often pictured battling against blizzards, in reality its habitat also included vast grasslands.

Its larger horn grew up to 33 inches long.

	Devonian 419-359 MYA	Carboniferous 359-299 MYA	Permian 299-252 MYA	Triassic 252-201 MYA	Jurassic 201-145 MYA	Cretaceous 145-66 MYA	Paleogene 66-23 MYA	Neogene 23-3 MYA
	Paleozoic 541-252 MYA			Mesozoic 252-66 MYA			Cenozoic 66-0 MYA	

SMILODON

Smy-LO-don

MEANING: "Knife tooth"
PERIOD: Neogene
LOCALITY: Northern Europe and Asia
LENGTH: 8.2 ft
WEIGHT: 617 lbs
DIET: Carnivore

Three species of *Smilodon* prowled the American continents during the Pleistocene and Holocene, including the *S. gracilis* and the bulky *S. populator*. They hunted camels, horses, and bison in North America, and in South America included now-extinct local herbivores like toxodonts in their diet.

Smilodon leaps from a tumble of rocks to launch itself at its prey.

CURVED CANINES

The enlarged canines that grew from *Smilodon*'s upper jaw were up to 11 inches long. It could open its mouth extremely wide to provide enough space for the canines to function, and it likely used them to deliver precise bites to the throat of its prey.

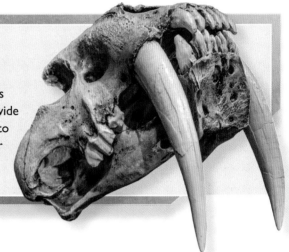

STICKY END

One of the world's most famous fossil sites is the La Brea tar pits in Los Angeles, which has preserved the remains of thousands of animals. One study of the remains showed that the injuries suffered by *Smilodon* were different from those inflicted on the dire wolf, another hunter of the time. *Smilodon* suffered almost twice as many injuries, suggesting ambush-style hunting was more dangerous than the chase-dominated strategy of the wolves.

Devonian	Carboniferous	Permian	Triassic	Jurassic	Cretaceous	Paleogene	Neogene
419-359 MYA	359-299 MYA	299-252 MYA	252-201 MYA	201-145 MYA	145-66 MYA	66-23 MYA	23-3 MYA
Paleozoic 541-252 MYA			Mesozoic 252-66 MYA			Cenozoic 66-0 MYA	

GLOSSARY

AETOSAUR: A **clade** of herbivorous **pseudosuchian**, which often possessed armor.

ANKYLOSAUR: A **clade** of **thyreophorans** with a body covered in armor.

ARCHOSAUR: A **clade** of very successful reptiles that includes the modern crocodilians and birds. It is split into two major groups, the avemetatarsalians and the pseudosuchians.

ARTHROPOD: A large **clade** of invertebrates with an **exoskeleton**, body segments, and paired limbs. This includes modern insects, arachnids, and crustaceans, as well their extinct relatives.

AVEMETATARSALIA: The **clade** of archosaurs that includes pterosaurs, dinosaurs, and modern birds.

BIPED: A **tetrapod** that moves around on only its hind limbs.

BRAINCASE: The bones of the skull that surround the brain and its tissues.

CEPHALODPOD: A **clade** of **invertebrates** that includes modern-day squid, octopus, and cuttlefish, and their extinct relatives.

CERATOPSIAN: A group of **marginocephalian** dinosaurs, famous for their horned or frilled skulls.

CERATOSAUR: A **clade** of primitive **theropods** that includes several species that survived to the end of the Cretaceous.

CLADE: A group of **organisms** that share a common ancestor.

COMPOUND EYES: Highly complex eyes seen in arthropods.

CONVERGENT EVOLUTION When two or more distantly related **organisms** independently evolve similar traits in order to adapt to similar environments or to perform similar functions. The wings of birds, bats, insects, and **pterosaurs** are an example.

CROCODILIAN: A **clade** that includes modern crocodiles, alligators, caimans, and gharials, as well as their closest extinct relatives.

DINOSAURIFORMES: A **clade** that includes **dinosaurs** and their closest relatives. These relatives possess some, but not all, the traits seen in their dinosaur cousins.

ENDOTHERMIC: an **organism** that is capable of generating heat internally, such as modern birds and mammals.

ERA: A large expanse of geological time, for example the **Mesozoic**. Eras are made up of several **periods**.

EUKARYOTES: More complex **organisms** that possess specialized structures to create energy, as well as housing their DNA within an internal membrane. All animals, plants, and fungi are eukaryotes.

EVOLUTION: The continual process by which life changes over time.

EXOSKELETON: A term used to describe the hard outer layers of various **organisms.**

EXTINCTION: When a **species** permanently dies out. Extinction happens all the time, but during mass extinctions, several species or entire **clades** can become extinct over a short time frame.

FOSSIL: The preservation of the remains or traces of an **organism** that have turned to stone.

GAIT: The way an animal moves its limbs.

GENE: A tiny section of DNA that codes for the building blocks of proteins. Hundreds of thousands of genes are found in a single strand of DNA.

GILL ARCH: Structures made of bone or cartilage that help support the gills.

HADROSAUR: A **clade** of **ornithopod** dinosaur that evolved in the Cretaceous and often sported showy crests.

HETERODONT: When an animal possesses two or more differently shaped sets of teeth in its jaws, which are used for different functions.

INSECTIVORE: An animal whose diet is mainly insects and kin.

INVERTEBRATE: Organisms that lack a backbone.

KERATIN: a tough protein that helps make the claws, scales and beaks or various **organisms**.

MANIRAPTORAN: A **clade** of advanced **theropods** that were closely related to modern birds.

MARGINOCEPHALIAN: A group of **ornithischians**, which includes the horned **ceratopsians** and the dome-headed **pachycephalosaurs**.

MESOZOIC: An **era** that spans from the **Triassic** to the **Cretaceous** and is sometimes referred to as "the age of the dinosaurs."

MULTICELLULAR ORGANISMS: Organisms made up of more than one cell.

NICHE: The role or position a species has in its ecosystem, which includes its interactions with other **organisms** as well as its environment.

GLOSSARY

OCELLI: The smaller "simple eyes" between the two larger **compound eyes** of various arthropods.

ORGANISM: A living thing.

ORNITHISCHIAN: One of the two major **clades** of dinosaurs, which included the **marginocephalians**, the **ornithopods**, and the **thyreophorans**. The other clade is the **saurischians**.

ORNITHOPOD: A hugely successful **ornithischian clade**. Several more advanced **species** possess extravagant bony crests.

OSTEODERMS: A type of bone that is embedded within the skin.

PACHYCEPHALOSAUR: A **clade** herbivorous **marginocephalian** dinosaurs famous for their thick, domed skulls.

PALAEOZOIC: The **era** before the Mesozoic.

PERIOD: A smaller unit of geological time that divides an **era**.

PHORUSRHACID: A **clade** of birds commonly known as the "terror birds." These were large, flightless predators that appeared after the extinction of the dinosaurs.

PHOTOSYNTHESIS: The chemical reaction that uses sunlight to create sugars, which is seen in some **prokaryotes** and all plants.

PHYTOSAUR: A clade of extinct **archosaurs** that looked similar to modern crocodilians due to **convergent evolution**.

PLACODERM: A several groups of extinct armored fish that patrolled the **Palaeozoic** seas. This is not a true clade, as they don't all descend from the same close common ancestor.

PROKARYOTES: Simple, single-celled **organisms** that include bacteria.

PROSAUROPOD: An informal name for several species of primitive **sauropodomorphs**. Several were bipedal and were replaced by the **sauropods**.

PSEUDOSUCHIA: One of the two major **clades** of **archosaurs** that includes modern crocodilians and their close extinct relatives.

PTEROSAUR: The family of flying reptiles that dominated the **Mesozoic** skies.

QUADRUPED: A **tetrapod** that moves around on all four limbs.

SAURISCHIAN: One of the two major dinosaur **clades**, which can be broken down into the **sauropomorphs** and **theropods**.

SAUROPOD: The more advanced group of **sauropodomorphs**. These were bigger and all were quadrupedal, evolving after the first **"prosauropods."**

SAUROPODOMORPH: The group of typically large, herbivorous **saurischian** dinosaurs. It included the early **"prosauropods"** and the more successful **sauropods**.

SCAVENGER: An animal that feeds on the carcasses of already dead animals. Most predators scavenge from time to time.

SPECIES: A particular type of **organism**, which is often able to breed with other individuals from its species.

STEGOSAUR: A **clade** of **thyreophoran** dinosaurs, whose backs and tails were lined with broad plates or spines.

SUPERCONTINENT: An enormous landmass made up of many continents that have collided together.

TEMNOSPONDYL: a clade of extinct amphibians that first evolved during the Carboniferous.

TETRAPOD: A **vertebrate** with four limbs.

TETRAPODOMORPH: A **clade** that includes **tetrapods** and their closest relatives. These relatives possess some, but not all, the traits seen in their tetrapod cousins.

THERAPSID: A large **clade** that includes modern mammals and their extinct relatives.

THEROPOD: One of the two major **clades** of **saurischian** dinosaurs, and the only one to survive to the present day. They were often carnivorous and **bipedal**, and include modern-day birds.

THYREOPHORAN: One of the major **ornithischian** groups, it includes the armored **ankylosaurs** and spiky **stegosaurs**.

TITANOSAUR: A **clade** of **sauropod** dinosaurs, often known for their extreme size. Several of these herbivores were the largest land animals to ever walk the Earth.

VERTEBRAE: The bones that make up the spinal column, which help support the animal.

VERTEBRATE: An **organism** with a spinal column made up of individual **vertebrae**.

INDEX

INDEX

The publishers would like to thank the following sources for their kind permission to reproduce the pictures and footage in this book. The numbers listed below give the page on which they appear in the book.
(T=top, B=bottom, L=left, R=right, C=centre)

Alamy: /AGF Srl: 35C; /agefotostock: 22BL; /BSIP SA: 10-11; /Classic Image: 70BL; /Corbin17: 135T, 139T, 147T; /dpa picture alliance archive: 39T; /DeAgostini/UIG: 37B; /Phil Degginger: 104B, 138T; /Dorling Kindersley Ltd: 42B, 48T, 53B, 64-65; /Eye Risk: 114-115; /Xavier Fores - Joana Roncero: 100B, 101T; /Chris Hellier: 39B; /Alfonso Fabio Iozzino: 143T; /R Kawka: 91R; / The Natural History Museum: 20BL, 26B, 65T, 85R, 89C; /Natural Visions: 84TL; /Roberto Nistri: 95R; /Panther Media GmbH: 93T; /Photo 12: 62C; /Q-Images: 117B; /REDA &CO srl: 80B; / Andrew Rubtsov: 148BR; /Stocktrek Images, Inc.: 14B, 19BL, 21, 40-41, 47TL, 55T, 111T; /Tom Wagner: 96B; /World History Archive: 79TL; /ZUMA Press, Inc.: 127B

Dmitry Bogdanov: 56

Getty Images: /breckeni: 34T; /Dorling Kindersley: 53R; /Education Images/UIG: 121T; /Mark Garlick/Science Photo Library: 144-145; /Walter Geiersperger: 81T; /Kevin Schafer: 52R; / Nobumichi Tamura/Stocktrek Images: 62-63

James Kuether Natural History Art: 36-37, 54B, 90, 110-111

RBINS: 54TR

Carola Radke/MfN: 25B

Science Photo Library: /Jaime Chirinos: 15T, 16-17, 91B, 146; /Herve Conge, ISM: 103B; / DeAgostini/UIG: 34B; /Carlos Goldin: 97B; /Roger Harris: 61TL; /Masato Hattori: 23T, 47B, 92T, 92B; /Mikkel Juul Jensen: 55B; /Michael Long: 26T; /Claus Lunau: 18-19, 19BR; /Walter Myers: 48B; /Natural History Museum, London: 88B, 89B; /Jose Antonio Penas: 57, 116-117; /Millard H. Sharp: 23B, 35B, 36B, 43T, 45T, 72B, 79R, 103T; /Gwen Shockey: 18B; /John Sibbick: 17T, 20T, 27, 49; /Roman Uchytell: 24-25, 147B, 151B

Shutterstock: /AuntSpray: 12-13, 12L, 150B; /Catmando: 20BR, 93B; /DM7: 72-73, 73B; /Dotted Yeti: 8-9, 14-15, 59T, 126-127, 127T; /Daniel Eskridge: 33R, 62T, 63T, 98-99, 99T, 115B, 150T; / frantic00: 62B; /Jean-Michel Girard: 33L; /Goldilock Project: 86-87; /Herschel Hoffmeyer: 22-23, 33TL, 52L, 94-95, 104-105, 105R, 140-141, 142-143, 149B; /Akkharat Jarusilawong: 131B; /Mark_ Kostich: 149T; /Matis75: 88-89; /Morphart Creation: 13R; /prapass: 33TR; /Nicolas Primola: 99B; / Janos Rautonen: 41R; /Reimar: 109T, 113B; /Michael Rosskothen: 38-39, 58L; /Albert Russ: 67T; / Sasha Samardzija: 151T; /Sipa: 61TR; /Smelov: 30-31; /Rattiya Thongdumhyu: 11T; /Bas van der Pluijm: 67B; /Sandy van Vuuren: 65B; /Warpaint: 15B, 42-43, 46B, 47TR, 58-59, 60-61, 70C, 96-97, 100-101, 112-113, 130L, 148L; /Wlad74: 71T; /Jolanta Wojcicka: 11B; /YuRi Photolife: 31T

Linda Snook/MBNMS: 16L

James St. John: 114B

Unsplash: /Pedro Lastra: 28-29

Welbeck Publishing: 112B; /Models created by Jiři Adamec: 3, 4-5, 6, 30B, 32, 33T, 33BL, 33BR, 44-45, 46L, 50-51, 66-67, 68-69, 74-75, 75T, 76-77, 78, 80-81, 82-83, 84-85, 102-103, 106-107, 108-109, 118-119, 120-121, 122-123, 124-125, 125B, 128-129, 130-131, 131R, 132-133, 134-135, 136-137, 139B

Every effort has been made to acknowledge correctly and contact the source and/or copyright holder of each picture, any unintentional errors or omissions will be corrected in future editions of this book.